A *Dazzle* of
DRAGONFLIES

A *Dazzle* of DRAGONFLIES

FORREST L. MITCHELL
Associate Professor

JAMES L. LASSWELL
Senior Research Associate

Texas Agricultural Experiment Station
Texas A & M University
Stephenville, Texas

A PETER N. NÉVRAUMONT BOOK

TEXAS A&M UNIVERSITY PRESS
College Station

Texas A&M University Press
College Station, Texas

Printed in P. R. China.

The paper used in this publication meets the minimum requirements of American National Standard for Information Sciences—Permanence of Paper for Printed Library Materials, ANSI Z39.48-1984.
♾

Library of Congress Cataloging-in-Publication Data

Mitchell, Forrest Lee, 1955-
  A dazzle of dragonflies / Forrest Mitchell, James Lasswell.
    p. cm.
  "A Peter N. Névraumont Book"
  Includes bibliographical references and index.
  ISBN 1-58544-459-6 (cloth : alk. paper)
  1. Dragonflies. I. Lasswell, James, 1942- II. Title.
  QL520.M58 2005
  595.7'33—DC22
                    2004024969

Jacket and book design by Cathleen Elliott

Created and Produced by
Névraumont Publishing Company
New York City

{FIGURE I}

The Neon Skimmer (Libellula croceipennis) *is found around small,*
shaded, spring-fed springs in the southwestern United States. The bright
red coloration of the face, thorax, and abdomen of the male help
distinguish it from the male Flame Skimmer, which is more orange-red
in color. Photo © James L. Lasswell.

{C O N T E N T S}

THE WORLD OF DRAGONFLIES

Creatures of the sunlight that pirouette on sparkling wings in plain view of all who take the time to look, dragonflies are nonetheless among the most elusive of insects. Few people get a close look at these ever-vigilant aerial predators, and fewer still know what they are seeing [Figure 2].

One of our goals in this book is to present the far-reaching and sometimes secret world of dragonflies, from their common appearance in folklore around the world to the intricacies of their life history and the technological advances in their study. Another goal is to introduce readers to the many ways they can continue to explore and develop their own interests in these extraordinary creatures.

The images in the book are meant to illustrate the dragonflies themselves, in order to display their exquisite color and variety, and to showcase them in their natural environment, where their beauty speaks for itself.

We hope, however, to spur the reader to do more than look at the pictures. Interaction with dragonflies can be quite entertaining and rewarding. It can also be used to catch the interest of children and increase their appreciation for these delightful insects. For those who want to pursue the study of dragonflies, we offer a range of activities to suit different tastes and levels of engagement, including watching dragonflies, counting migrants, making a water garden to attract dragonflies, creating dragonfly images for display, collecting dragonflies, and rearing larvae. We urge you to get outside and try some of these yourself.

Because the insect order Odonata, to which dragonflies and damselflies belong, is not well studied compared with other animal groups, authoritative manuals on dragonflies and damselflies that could be read and understood by the casual or untrained observer were scarce until recently. Even

{FIGURE 2}

A male Mayan Setwing (Dythemis maya) *faces the camera in a typical setwing pose, alert to its surroundings and ready for instant flight. Found mainly in Mexico, this dragonfly species crosses the border into the Big Bend area of West Texas. Photo © Greg W. Lasley.*

Sparkling Jewelwing (Calopteryx dimidiata), *a damselfly. Photo © James L. Lasswell.*

into the 1990s, the most comprehensive guide to dragonflies (damselflies were not treated) was from 1955. Books with color pictures were usually obsolete or hard to find. To make matters even more difficult, dragonflies are hard to collect and usually unimpressive as collection specimens. Dried, pinned dragonflies lose most of their color and become extremely fragile—collected specimens must be kept in plastic envelopes to keep disengaged parts together in the same location.

With the arrival of the information age, these difficulties began to be circumvented by better photographic technology and digital imagery. Dragonfly hobbyists, an esoteric group, could begin to find one another without thought to geographical distances. Internet websites, then books, began to follow as interest in the Odonata species grew and more information became available.

In the mid-1990s, while wrestling with the challenges of identifying dragonflies and damselflies for a water-quality project we were working on, we stumbled on the technique of using a flatbed scanner to acquire images of living adult dragonflies and damselflies. The full-color scans could be made reasonably quickly—a necessity because these animals do not willingly remain still—and be almost instantly available in digital form for review. Photographic skills were not required and a failed scan could be redone immediately on the same specimen without waiting for film to develop. These scans were very useful to us in our scientific study, but they also displayed the full effect of dragonflies in living color. Most people never see the beauty the scans revealed for a number of reasons, not the least of which is the capricious and aloof nature of the dragonflies themselves.

We resolved to display our images to the online community, and on September 1, 1996, we introduced the Digital Dragonflies Project to the Internet at www.dragonflies.org. Acceptance was immediate, and the project quickly expanded. A number of superb photographers, some of whose work appears in this book, became contributors to the site, now one of the largest online collections of dragonfly images in the world.

An unexpected offshoot of the website was the mail we received from a number of people who wrote and asked questions about dragonflies and damselflies. Over the years, the quantity of mail became so voluminous, and from enough geographical locations, that we could see the need for a book about dragonflies that was neither a field guide nor a detailed scientific treatise. With the encouragement of our correspondents and the people we have met through our presentations at various nature clubs and bird festivals, we wrote this book to promote greater understanding of dragonflies, and thereby increase interest and foster satisfaction in becoming engaged with these fascinating animals. Since our experience is mainly with North American dragonflies, the book focuses on these. While damselflies are no less interesting, they are not treated in this book except in occasional points of interest or in comparisons with dragonflies [Figure 3].

Chapters two and three, on folklore and prehistory, address the questions we often receive about these topics, especially those about the various names for dragonflies in other cultures and those about the giant prehistoric dragonflies. Chapters four and five, "Dragonfly Lives" and "The Natural History of Dragonflies," give an overview of these topics so that the reader may be better prepared for the real life encounters with dragonflies in the remaining chapters. "Watching Dragonflies" in chapter six discusses this recent trend among amateur and expert naturalists alike, brought about mainly by the development of close-focus binoculars and the recent publication of some good regional field guides. "Collecting Dragonflies," chapter seven, gives basic instruction for making a classical insect collection, including tips for collecting, preserving, and storing.

The information in chapter eight, "Water Gardening for Dragonflies," is in response to the many questions we receive about how to attract dragonflies to gardens and backyards. The popularity of butterfly gardening has increased in recent years, and dragonflies, which are no less colorful or interesting, are certainly candidates for similar treatment. We also discuss rearing dragonfly larvae captured in water gardens or ponds. Chapter nine is about acquiring images of dragonflies and includes a detailed description of the scanning technique used for the high resolution images in this book. We also explain photographic methods of capturing dragonflies with both digital and film cameras.

The Digital Dragonflies website will continue to serve as a forum for questions and a place to find additional detail beyond the scope and page limits of this book. We want you to have as much fun interacting with dragonflies as we have and hope to see you online at www.dragonflies.org.

CHAPTER TWO

DRAGONFLY TALES

The myths and folklore surrounding dragonflies have a special fascination for many people. We are often asked where the name "dragonfly" came from, for example. Do they sting? Are they are poisonous? A host of other questions that fall generally into the category of dragonfly myths or folklore come to us. The origins of most dragonfly lore are beyond our expertise as entomologists, but in this chapter we take a brief look at the dragonfly as it is viewed in myth and legend around the world.

The following perspective by James reflects the experiences of both of us growing up in rural Texas.

My parents passed on to me their beliefs about dragonflies as part of the day-to-day happenings on our family farm in north-central Texas, but they never said, "What I am about to tell you now is part of the folklore of the dragonfly." Instead, I grew up mistakenly thinking that the folklore and the reality of dragonflies were one and the same.

Our farm was remote and primitive by today's standards. We did not get electricity until I was a little over nine years old, and during the hot summer months, we would often eat our noon and evening meals on our large front porch to avoid the stifling heat inside the house. On many of these occasions, I recall seeing groups of large insects darting about in the open area in front of the porch, their bodies outlined in the early evening light. My parents called them "mosquitohawks," one of the more commonly used names for dragonflies in the United States. I would go out and watch the mosquitohawks feed on smaller insects, which, since these were mosquitohawks, I assumed were mosquitoes.

My father used to tell my brother, sister, and me that when these large swarms gathered it was going to rain soon. (Similar beliefs can also be found in the dragonfly folklore of China, France, and Japan.) He also told us that you could tell how much it

{FIGURE 4}

A "snake doctor," in this case a male Eastern Pondhawk (Erythemis simplicicollis), *perched on a fishing pole: a sure sign that the angler will soon get a bite. Photo © James L. Lasswell.*

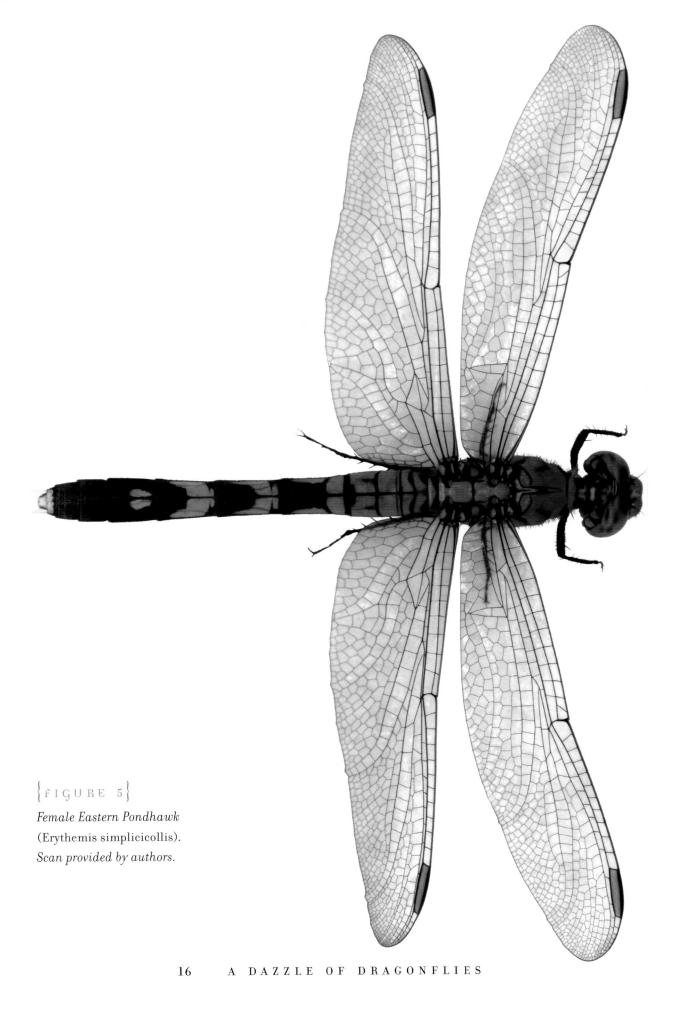

{FIGURE 5}

Female Eastern Pondhawk
(Erythemis simplicicollis).
Scan provided by authors.

would rain by how high the mosquitohawks were flying. High-flying ones foretold a heavy rain; low-flying ones, a light rain. Of course it did not always rain after each of these sightings, but it did rain often enough that we chose to forget the times it didn't and were duly impressed by our father's knowledge.

One thing that puzzled me, though, was when we went fishing, which we did quite often, the same insects that swarmed in front of our house were suddenly referred to as "snake doctors" by my parents and "devil's needles" or "devil's darning needles" by my maternal grandparents. We were always reminded that when a snake doctor landed on our pole, or on our float, we would soon get a bite *[Figure 4]*.

According to the following poem from Lafcadio Hearn's *A Japanese Miscellany* (1901), the Japanese apparently considered the opposite to be true.

**Tsuri-beta no
Sao ni kite Neru
Tombo kana!**
*(See! The dragonfly settles down to sleep on
the rod of the unskilled angler!)*

In the fall of 2002, I met two fishermen at Falcon Lake, located along the Texas-Mexico border, who carried this idea of getting a bite when a snake doctor landed on their poles even further. They claimed that if one of the green ones landed—probably a female Eastern Pondhawk (*Erythemis simplicicollis*) *[Figure 5]*—they were assured of catching a channel catfish (*Ictalurus punctatus*) and if a red dragonfly landed—probably a male Variegated Meadowhawk (*Sympetrum corruptum*) *[Figure 6]*—they would catch a blue catfish (*Ictalurus furcatus*).

My grandmother was absolutely sure that "devil's darning needles" were poisonous (they are not) and often admonished my brother and me for trying to catch one. She told us that if they stung us we would be sick for a long time and might even die. We commonly found poisonous snakes on our farm so we were not terribly concerned about the devil's darning needles; however, our efforts to catch one were never successful.

On a trip to Madison, Wisconsin in July of 2000, I realized just how widespread my grandmother's views of dragonflies were, at least in the United States. We walked along State Street—a street of shops, bars, and restaurants that extends for more than a mile

Male Variegated Meadowhawk (Sympetrum corruptum). *Photo © James L. Lasswell.*

from the state capitol building to the university campus. I suddenly heard a commotion a short distance away from me. I turned to see a group of college students swatting vigorously at the air above their heads. At first I thought they were swatting at a wasp, but then I spotted a mated pair of dragonflies.

As luck would have it, the pair flew over and landed on my shoulder. While the dragonflies rested there, one of the students said, "Those things will sting you." It sounded just like my grandmother! I gently slid the index finger of my right hand under the pair of dragonflies and held them out in front of me so that I could see them better, and I observed to the group that they were only dragonflies. Another student said, "those things are poisonous" (my grandmother again), and they moved slowly away from me, looking back occasionally to see, I presume, if I had met an untimely death from the two dragonflies still perched on my finger. The dragonflies soon tired of their perch and flew up to land on the rough stone face of the building above us.

My parents and grandparents passed along to me dragonfly names and superstitions, which were surely taught to them by their own parents or grandparents. What about those college students in Madison? Had their beliefs been passed on to them from their parents or grandparents? What about the two fishermen from Falcon Lake? It is definitely conceivable that they came up with the idea that the color of dragonfly on their fishing poles determined the kind of fish they were going to catch. Could this be the origin of a new local superstition? Could be! New dragonfly folklore? Possibly!

Dragonflies, though the subject of many stories, poems, and legends, have not always enjoyed as positive an image as some other insects throughout the world. Butterflies and honeybees are regularly recognized in song, story, or verse for their beauty and contributions to humanity. Dragonflies, although revered in Asia and some Native American cultures, have generally been viewed with superstition in the United States and in Europe since the Middle Ages. During that period, people in some parts of Europe believed the devil could take on any earthly form he chose. The fly was thought to be one of his favorites, and eventually the fly became synonymous with the devil himself. The dragonfly's reputation (a large fly in the mind of some) in Europe and then the United States has suffered because of this association.

The Dragonfly in United States Folklore

The words "dragonfly" and "mosquito-hawk" are surely the most widely used terms for this large winged insect in the United States. Butterflies, flies, gnats, midges, damselflies, other dragonflies, swarming ants (including fire ants), and a host of other flying insects fall prey to the ravenous dragonfly. Many people think mosquitoes, because they are so plentiful and reside in the same habitats as dragonflies, are a large part of the dragonfly's diet. Since dragonflies eat so many insects that are troublesome or harmful to humans, Charles A. R. Campbell, the author of *Bats, Mosquitoes, and Dollars* (1925), called the dragonfly "man's best friend in the insect world." His work with bats, mosquitoes, and dragonflies is thought to have contributed a great deal to the fight against malaria, a mosquito-born disease.

The names "snake doctor" and "snake feeder" are common in some midwestern and southern states and also in England. Most freshwater habitats in the United States have an abundance of both snakes and dragonflies, and a snake's head protruding above the waterline must surely make an inviting perch for a tired dragonfly. Additionally, female dragonflies often lay their eggs near limbs, rocks, or practically anything extending above the water. Observations of a dragonfly laying eggs near a snake, or of dragonflies landing on or trying to land on a snake's head, could easily have given rise to these terms since the dragonfly would appear to be "tending" the snake. This "tending of snakes" has been carried even further in the southern United States. Here dragonflies are seen as servants of snakes and are believed to be able to revive them, Lazarus-like, from the dead.

European influence is evident in the monikers "devil's needle" and "devil's darning needle." According to folklore, dragonflies in this guise are capable of all sorts of dastardly deeds. In many parts of the United States, people believe they have a poisonous sting (they do not). In Iowa, devil's darning needles sew together the fingers or toes of a person who falls asleep within its reach. In Kansas, they may sew up the mouths of scolding women, saucy children (parents must love this), and profane men. Even more sinister is the belief that the devil's darning needle will enter a person's ear and penetrate the brain.

"Devil's horse" is a name derived from similar names for the dragonfly in some European countries (see the discussion below). In several midwestern states, the dragonfly is referred to as "St. George's horse," "Dickens' horse," "Dickerson's horse," and "Dickerson's mare." The latter three names arose because among the early settlers the words Dickens or Dickerson were synonymous with the word devil.

The Dragonfly in Native American Folklore

Among Native American tribes, the dragonfly is considered to be flighty and carefree,

This photograph of an Indian pictograph was taken at The Nature Conservancy's Dolan Falls Preserve in the arid lands of southwest Texas. In the upper right corner of the photo, in red, is the symbol used by many western Indians to depict the dragonfly. This particular pictograph was found along the face of a rock wall just above a series of springs that flow from the base of the wall into Dolan Creek. Photo © James L. Lasswell.

symbolizing swiftness and activity. According to the Navajo story of emergence, the Tanilai' (dragonfly) was one of the original twelve "people," along with the dark ants, red ants, yellow beetles, hard beetles, stone-carrier beetles, black beetles, coyote-dung beetles, white-faced beetles, bats, locusts, and white locusts. These people came to life at a place called House Made of Red Rock. Dragonflies appear in some dry (sand) paintings from Navajo ritual ceremonies where they are often shown around a pool of water, symbolizing the water's purity.

{ FIGURE 8, *opposite* }

A beautiful bowl by Zuni artist Priscilla Peynetsa. Although this piece is modern, it reflects the artistry of the Zunis and their connection to the creatures of nature. Image courtesy of ElkRidgeArt.com, Evergreen, Colorado. Photo © Lee Hovey King.

{ FIGURE 8a, *above* }

This pottery cornmeal basket is by the Zuni artist Noreen Simplicio. A wonderful example of the use of the dragonfly in Zuni culture, the basket is now in the collection of Robin Sechrist, Denver, Colorado. Image courtesy of ElkRidgeArt.com, Evergreen, Colorado. Photo © Anne Goldstein.

In Hopi rock art the symbol for the dragonfly is a single vertical line with two (sometimes only one) horizontal cross lines [Figure 7]. These can be found in the Hopi Mesas in Arizona, in Zion National Park in Utah, and in the kiva murals in the Awatovi and Kawaika-a ruins in Arizona. This type of symbolism is also present in a number of cross necklaces made by the Pueblo and Navajo peoples. Dragonfly emblems were also popular in Native American pottery and are still used today [Figures 8, 8a].

One of the most delightful dragonfly folktales comes from the Zunis in New Mexico. This story was first recorded in 1883 by Frank Hamilton Cushing for the Bureau of American Ethnology. Cushing's translations of some of the Zuni folktales were published in 1975 in the book *Zuni Breadstuff*. The second chapter, "The Origin of the Dragonfly and of the Corn Priests, or Guardian of the Seeds," goes something like this:

A young boy and his sister fell asleep and were accidentally forgotten when their parents and the rest of the villagers abandoned their village in hard times to find food. As time passed, the young boy made a toy insect out of corn and grasses to try to comfort his younger sister. The toy, called the "corn-being" by the Zunis, came to life and was eventually assigned by the gods (who lived in the Dance Hall of the Dead) to teach the children their duties so that the gods would favor them. But the little girl became very ill, and the corn-being flew to the south and sought the Maidens of Corn (also called Mother Maidens and Mothers of the Seed) that they might come and comfort her and her brother. When they arrived, the Maidens of Corn blessed the children with food and told the boy that he and his sister were beloved among the gods and that his sister would become the mother of their people and the boy would become the father of their people. Eventually the people of the village returned. The boy and his sister became great leaders, and because the gods favored them their people were blessed.

Toward the end of the story, the corn-being asked the boy to make another of his form and to call them and their offspring "dragonfly." The boy did this and told the dragonfly the following:

"Thy form in remembrance will I paint on the sacred things, emblematic of spring and the health-giving rains of springtime and thy companion shall I paint, the symbol of summer and the pools of summer showers."

To this day the black, white, and red dragonfly comes in early summer when the corn tassels bloom. He flies from one plant to another, never content with his resting place. Following him comes the beautiful green dragonfly, the corn-being's companion. Fashioned from a corn plant, the dragonfly is green and yellow, like a stalk of growing corn in the sunlight.

In 1986, Tony Hillerman wrote a version of this story in his book, *The Boy Who Made Dragonfly: A Zuni Myth.* In 1991, Kristina

Rodanas wrote a children's version entitled *Dragonfly's Tale.*

The Dragonfly in European Folklore

According to German folklore, the dragonfly originated in Germany, but two other European folktales place the mythical origin of the dragonfly in Romania. In each of these tales the dragonfly's origin is associated with black magic or the devil, reflecting many Europeans' belief that the dragonfly was evil. Swedes, for example, believed that the dragonfly was used by the devil to weigh people's souls. Supposedly, if a dragonfly repeatedly flew around someone's head, it was weighing his or her soul and that person could then expect some great injury.

The German folktale that places the mythical origin of the dragonfly in Germany coins the name *Hatzpferd* (hunting horse), an appellation for the dragonfly that is still in use in Germany today. Eden Emanuel Sarot told the story, recapped here, in his book *Folklore of the Dragonfly: A Linguistic Approach* (1958).

There was once a young princess who led a rather wild life. She cared only for herself and spent her days dashing about on her fiery steed, caring not what she destroyed. One day as she was riding through the dark forest, a little man approached her and spoke to her in a polite voice. But the hard-hearted princess did not wish to stop and ordered him out of her way. Unfortunately, he did not heed her order, and she spurred her horse and rode over him. Having been treated in this manner, the little man shouted after her, "May you always be joined to your horse as one!" Almost immediately the princess and her horse were changed into a winged insect, which to this day is called *Hatzpferd* in remembrance of what had happened.

Sarot theorized that the English name "dragonfly" might have come from an interesting Romanian folktale about the origin of the dragonfly, in which the devil played a major role.

There was, in ancient times, a great deal of strife (as one might expect) between God and the devil.

The devil, being the devil, always wanted things his way and was constantly striving to gain material possessions. God grew tired of this constant conflict and decided to let the devil have his way for a while. He granted him wish after wish, but the devil, again being the devil, was never satisfied. The more he got, the more he wanted. Finally, God decided that enough was enough, and he sent an army of angels led by St. George to defeat the devil. God gave each of the angels a magnificent horse to ride into battle, but as St. George led the charge, his horse suddenly stopped and began to back up. He backed into the mounts upon which the angels were riding, and the army was soon in disarray. God, seeing what was happening, instructed St. George to dismount immediately, for his horse was possessed by the devil. St. George followed God's instructions, and as soon as he dismounted, his horse turned into a winged insect and flew away.

In Romania, the winged insect in the tale is called *calul dracului* (devil's horse) and *calul de Sf. George* (St. George's horse). "Dragonfly" may have stemmed from the Romanian word *drac,* which means both "devil" and "dragon." It is easy to see how St. George's horse, which turned into a flying insect under control of the devil (*drac*), could eventually end up as a *drac* (dragon) fly, thus explaining the origin of the English word dragonfly.

A second Romanian folktale about the origin of the dragonfly also features the devil as the main character. In this story, the devil walked the shoreline of a large lake, but he wanted to get to the other side. He spotted a fisherman in a boat only a short distance from shore and called to him to ask for a ride to the other side of the lake. The fisherman, seeing that it was the devil calling, immediately began to row away as fast as he could. The devil decided to get to the other shore by changing into an insect and flying. The devil took the form of the dragonfly. His arms and legs were changed to wings and his pointed tail became the dragonfly's long body. In this form he flew to the other side of the lake.

Probably the most popular names for the dragonfly in Europe are direct translations of "dragonfly" and also variations on the scientific name *Libellula,* a genus in the family Libellulidae (the largest family of dragonflies). There has been some disagreement regarding the origin of the name *Libellula.* Some feel it recalls a dragonfly's wings held straight out to the side when at rest, looking similar to the pages of an open book or *libel.* Others feel the name was derived from the word *libella* or "balancing scales." The word *libella* brings to mind the gentle rocking of the wings when a dragonfly is at rest or hovering over the water. Whatever the case, the names *libellule* (France), *Libelle* (Germany), *libelula* (Spain), and *libelinha* (Portugal) are among the most commonly used. The English name "balance fly" also evokes a similar image.

Since the dragonfly spends most of its life in and around water, colloquial names such as *Wasserjungfer* and *Wasserpfrau* (water nymph and water peacock—German), *water-juffer* (water nymph—Dutch), *nymphe* (water spirit—French), *cura-pess* (keeper of the fish—Italian), and *guarda-cibbia* (guard of the tubs—Italian) have cropped up. The last of

{ꜰ ɪ ɢ ᴜ ʀ ᴇ 9}

A teneral (newly emerged) Jade Clubtail (Arigomphus submedianus) *with its old "husk" (the exuvia) still attached to the rock at left. Photo © Curtis E. Williams.*

these evokes images of dragonflies keeping vigil over small washtubs in the yard. Several species of dragonflies will actually reproduce in watering troughs used for farm animals, in birdbaths, or even in containers as small as washtubs or water-filled buckets.

While dragonflies occasionally assume the names of other animals, such as *grilli* (cricket) in Italy, the most common animal in the colloquial names for dragonflies in Europe is the horse. Like the Romanian folktale's "devil's horse," we have *cavallo d'o demo* or *cavallo-das-bruxas* (witch's horse) in Portugal, *pirum hevoinen* in Finland, *chevau du diable* in France, and *caballito del diablo* (devil's little horse) in Spain. More endearing horse names include *peerdeken* (our dear little horse) from northern Belgium, *Goldspierken* (little golden horse) from Germany, and a number of others that refer to the dragonfly as "God's horse," "little horse," or "golden horse." Probably the most creative of these is the German designation *Pierd und Wagen,* or "horse and wagon."

The long, slender shape of the dragonfly has given rise to several names that include the words snake, knife, sword, needle, or some other type of sharp instrument. In France, for example, the dragonfly has been dubbed *aiguillette,* and in Italy *mattassaro,* both of which mean "needle." A number of European words depicts the dragonfly as doing harm to humans or animals, including the Norwegian *ore-sting* ("ear piercer") and the English *bullstang* or "bull sticker." Sometimes the dragonfly is personified, such as in France where it can be called "young married woman" (*mariee*), "little nun" (*moungeto*), and even "dressmaker" (*couturiere*). For many other fascinating names for dragonflies from Europe and around the world see Appendix B.

No discussion of the dragonfly in Europe should end without including this popular verse by Alfred (Lord) Tennyson *[Figure 9].*

Today I saw the dragon-fly
Come from the wells where he did lie.
An inner impulse rent the veil
Of his old husk: from head to tail
Came out clear plates of sapphire mail.
He dried his wings: like gauze they grew;
Thro' crofts and pastures wet with dew
A living flash of light he flew.
— "The Two Voices" (1883), lines 8–15

Visit a pond at twilight or early in the morning, and you may be rewarded with the opportunity to see what the famous poet described so well. Walk near that same pond during mid-morning, and you may see several newly emerged dragonflies arise from the shoreline vegetation, their wings now strong enough to fly short distances but still shiny, still delicate, still looking much like "clear plates of sapphire mail."

Maybe Tennyson sat on a warm summer morning at dawn and watched a dragonfly poke its head from the water and then select a suitable place for its emergence into adulthood. Perhaps Tennyson watched as the dragonfly forced its way out of the "old husk" that covered it—first the thorax, legs, and head, then the abdomen—and marveled as the delicate new wings became visible. The dragonfly's wings are bright and shiny, with a bluish metallic sheen, and very fragile right after emergence. The newly emerged dragonfly cannot fly effectively for a short period after its wings are fully expanded—"like gauze they grew"—but Tennyson surely waited and watched as the dragonfly dried its wings and launched itself skyward, appearing much like "a living flash of light" as it made its maiden flight across the pond.

The Dragonfly in Japanese Folklore

One of the old names of Japan is *Akitsu-shima,* or Island of the Dragonfly. According to Japanese folklore, it was so named some 2,600 years ago because the Emperor Jimmu, while gazing down upon the province of Yamato, observed that the land looked like a dragonfly licking its tail. Thus the province of Yamato became known as The Land of the Dragonfly, and this name was eventually extended to include the whole island. This reference to Yamato was later recognized in a poem by Emperor Jomei (AD 563–641), the thirty-fourth emperor of Japan. The translation is from the book *Country of Eight Islands: An Anthology of Japanese Poetry* by Hiroaki Sato and Burton Watson (1981).

Yamato has clusters of mountains but closest to the city is heavenly Mount Kagu. I climb; I stand and survey the land: Smoke rises in the countryside,

Gulls rise over the lake. A good land, this, the island of the dragonfly, the land of Yamato.

The dragonfly, an emblem of the country of Japan, was also known as *katsumushi* (the invincible insect), a favorite symbol of strength among Japanese warriors. During the seventeenth-century Tokugawa shogunate period, dragonflies were used as a motif for decorations on warriors' helmets.

Dragonflies are thought to bring good luck in Japan. This is evident in the folktale called "Dragonfly Choja" found in *Ancient Tales in Modern Japan: An Anthology of Japanese Folktales* by Fanny Hagin Mayer (1985). It is a story about a young, hardworking farmer who took a noontime nap (he and his wife had been working on a mountainside garden). While he was napping his wife saw a dragonfly come flying from the foot of the mountain and circle above the man's head and around his open mouth three times. When he awoke he said he had a dream that he was drinking some excellent wine. His wife told him about the dragonfly, and the two of them went around the mountain and found a clear spring flowing from below a rock. It was a spring of wine. The same mountain yielded an endless amount of gold, and the farmer and his wife became rich.

Thereafter he was called Danbury Choja because a *danbury*, which meant dragonfly in Oshu (an ancient name for the northern part of Japan), had shown him how to become a *choja* (millionaire). To become a *choja*, he had to possess treasure bestowed by heaven.

The ancient Japanese names *akitsu* and *akitsu-mushi* both mean "autumn insect" and are still used to refer to all the dragonflies of Japan. Although dragonflies fly throughout the summer months in Japan, they appear in great numbers in autumn, especially the red-colored *Sympetrum* species (meadowhawks), the ones most commonly written about in Japanese poetry. The colloquial name *aka-tombo*, *aka* meaning red and *tombo* meaning dragonfly, is actually used for many different species of red dragonflies found in Japan, including *Sympetrum* species. Kaya Shirao (1738?–1791) wrote the following haiku, from Lafcadio Hearn's *A Japanese Miscellany*, which conveys the association of the red dragonfly, *aka-tombo*, with the coming of autumn.

Aki no ki no
Aka-tombo Ni
Sadamarinu.
(That the autumn season has begun is decided by the [appearance of the] red dragonfly.)

The modern names for dragonflies in Japan are *yamma*, usually used to refer to the species in the family Aeshnidae (darners), and *tombo*, used to refer to all other Odonata, including both dragonflies and damselflies. The common names of dragonflies in Japan now consist of a prefix, in the form of one or more descriptive adjectives, and a suffix, which is always either Yamma or Tombo.

In *A Japanese Miscellany*, Lafcadio Hearn refers to a dragonfly known as Mugiwara-Tombo, the Wheat-Straw Dragonfly. Mugiwara-Tombo is a colloquial name used for the immature male and female *Orthetrum albistylum speciosum*. The mature male of this species is called Shiokara-Tombo, the Salt-Fish Dragonfly. *Shiokara* is a preparation of fish preserved in salt, and the mature male Salt-Fish Dragonfly has a white tail that looks very much like it has been dipped in salt.

The largest dragonfly in Japan, *Anotogaster sieboldii*, is now placed in the family

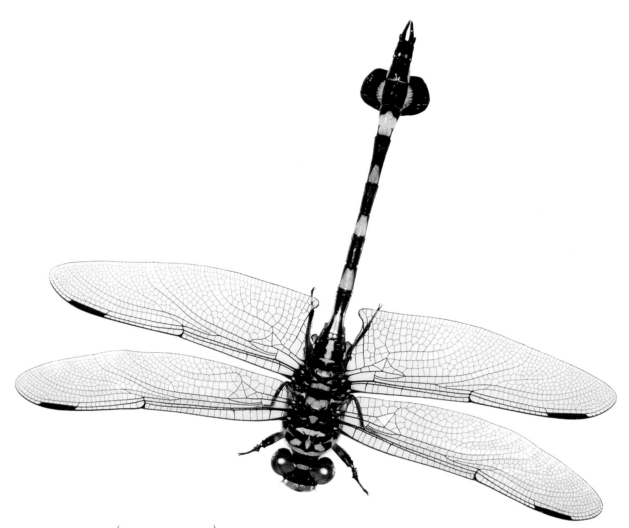

The Fan Aeshnid (Sinictinogomphus clavatus) *is not a member of the family Aeshnidae but of the family Gomphidae, from Japan. It has a large fan-like expansion of the eighth abdominal segment. Photo © Mitsutoshi Sugimura.*

Cordulegastridae but was once included in the family Aeshnidae and is still called Yamma or Oni-Yamma (Devil Aeshnid or Devil Dragonfly). Also still in use are the common names Ko-Oni-Yamma (Smaller Oni-Yamma, *Sieboldius albardae*) and Uchiwa-Yamma (Fan Aeshnid, *Sinictinogomphus clavatus*),

both of which now belong to the family Gomphidae *[Figure 10]*.

There are two species of dragonflies found in Japan that are thought to have changed little since their appearance in the odonate fauna millions of years ago. One of these is *Tanypteryx pryeri*, once considered to belong in the family Aeshnidae because of its size. Now placed in the family Petaluridae (petaltails), it is still known by the common name Mukashi-Yamma (Ancient Aeshnid).

Perhaps the most interesting dragonfly in Japan is the *Epiophlebia superstes* or Mukashi-Tombo (Ancient Dragonfly) *[Figures 11, 11a].* Fairly common in Japan, it is one of only two species of dragonflies in the world that belong to the "ancient" suborder Anisozygoptera.

Other names have been assigned to species of dragonflies because of their color. Aka-Tombo (red dragonfly) and Kino-Tombo (yellow dragonfly) are clearly named for their predominant color; however, Beni-Tombo (pink dragonfly) requires some explanation because *beni* does not mean pink. Japanese women use pink or reddish rouge, called *beni,* to color their cheeks and lips, thus the name Beni-Tombo, a bright pink dragonfly with the scientific name *Trithemis aurora.*

The only dragonfly species whose geographic range spans the globe, our Wandering Glider (*Pantala flavescens*), is known by names such as Shorai-Tombo (Dragonfly of the Dead) or Bon-Tombo

[Figure 12]. These dragonflies appear in large numbers about August 15th, a day of great religious significance among Buddhists, when the Hotoke-Sama (August Spirits of the Ancestors) are believed to revisit their former homes to be reunited with their families. This summer festival is called *Bon.*

During this time, the Shorai-Tombo or Bon-Tombo are thought to serve as winged mounts for the spirits as they return. Children are forbidden to molest any dragonfly, especially those that may happen to enter the family dwelling. To guide the ancestral souls back to their former homes, the family lights a small bonfire outside the house, usually in the garden. This welcoming flame is called the *mukae-bi.* When the Festival of Bon ends, the visiting souls are sent off with another bonfire, called *okuri-bi.* In some areas of Japan, small lanterns are released to float downriver or into the sea as part of this *okuri-bi* ritual.

The oldest recorded Japanese poem about dragonflies dates back about 1,400 years ago. Its composition is attributed to the Emperor Yuriaku (457-490) who wrote the poem in honor of a dragonfly

{FIGURE 11}

The Ancient Dragonfly (Epiophlebia super-stes), a male, from Japan. Photo © Mitsutoshi Sugimura.

{FIGURE 11a}

Side view of a male Ancient Dragonfly (Epiophlebia superstes), from Japan. Photo © Mitsutoshi Sugimura.

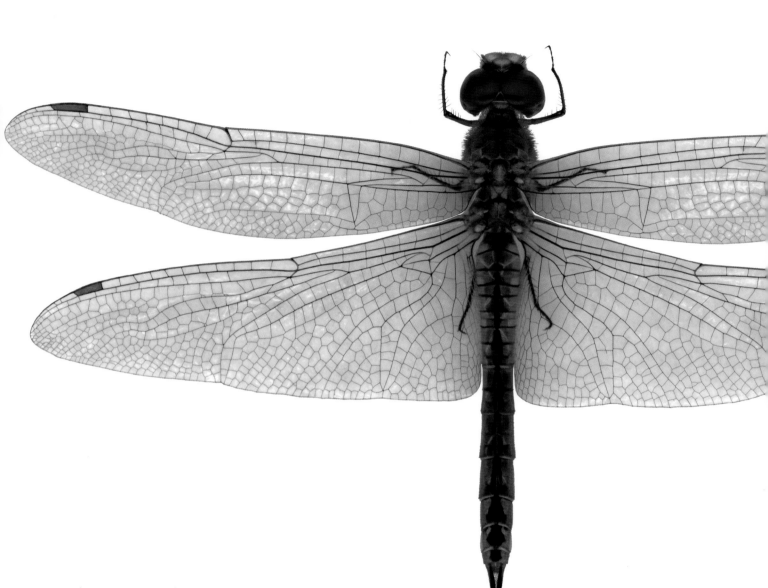

{FIGURE 12}

Known as the Dragonfly of the Dead in Japan,
Pantala flavescens (Wandering Glider), is the
only dragonfly whose geographic range cir-
cumnavigates the globe. Scan provided by
authors.

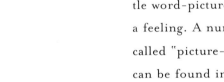

devouring a gadfly that bit him on the arm while he was hunting [*Figure 13*]. The last few lines of the poem, from Lafcadio Hearn's *A Japanese Miscellany*, refer again to Japan's long association with dragonflies.

Even the creeping insect
Waits upon the Great Lord:
Thy form it will bear,
O Yamato, Land of the Dragonfly!

Most Japanese poetry about dragonflies is in a short form of poetry called a *hokku* or more recently a *haiku*, a short, rhymeless poem that can easily be uttered in a single breath. The haiku is supposed to be a little word-picture that revives a memory or a feeling. A number of these, what Hearn called "picture-poems about dragonflies," can be found in his book and in the book by Hiroaki Sato and Burton Watson, *From the Country of Eight Islands*.

Among the greatest of the Japanese haiku poets was Matsuo Basho (1644–1694). Commonly referred to as Basho, he traveled throughout Japan teaching and judging poetry contests. In 1689 he wrote the following haiku about a dragonfly, from Sato and Watson's book:

Dragonfly unable to get hold of a grass blade

Frequently, you will see a dragonfly trying to find a place to land. It will move from one potential perching spot to another, often landing for just an instant as if it cannot find a spot where it feels comfortable.

Most of the old haiku masters like Basho showed a profound respect for life in their poetry. A student of Basho's, Takarai Kikaku (1661–1707), strayed from this principle when he wrote this poem, which has been freely interpreted on the Internet:

Darting dragonfly
pull off its wings, and look
crimson pepper pod.

He was admonished by Basho who warned that in Kikaku's verse life had been destroyed. Basho proceeded to rewrite the poem by simply turning the words around.

Crimson pepper pod
add two pairs of wings, and look
darting dragonfly.

Hearn recorded a number of appealing "picture poems" about dragonflies written by unknown Japanese poets.

Tombo no
Mo ya iri-hi no
Issekai.

(Dance, O dragonflies, in your world of the setting sun.)

The Chalk-fronted Corporal (Libellula julia) *eating an insect. Photo © Dave Westover.*

**Yukiote,
Dochiramo soreru
Tombo kana!**

(Meeting in flight, how wonderfully do the dragonflies glance away from each other!)

The old masters must surely have spent a great deal of time observing the activities of dragonflies in nature to have written such simple yet insightful poetry about these beautiful insects. The latter of these poems brings to mind the quick, darting motions of dragonflies in flight that have given rise to the Japanese word *tombogaeri* or "somersault." Literally translated *tombogaeri* means "dragonfly turning."

Catching dragonflies has been a favorite pastime for the children of Japan for hundreds of years. The chase and headlong abandon of the young hunters have been immortalized in numerous poems. Among these is the haiku, from Hearn:

**Hadaka-go no
Tombo tsuri-keri
Hiru no tsuji!**

*(The naked child has been catching dragonflies at the road
crossing, heedless of the noon sun!)*

Another is this touching poem by Chiyo
of Kaga, after the death of her son.

**Tombo-tsuri!
Kyo wa doko made
Itta yara!**

(Catching dragonflies! I wonder where he has gone today!)

In *A Japanese Miscellany*, Hearn describes a
very unusual device for catching dragonflies
used by the children of the province of Kii.
It consisted of a long hair with a very small
pebble attached to each end, forming a tiny
bola. The bola was thrown high into the air
(near a dragonfly of course), and when the
dragonfly grabbed either of the pebbles, the
hair twisted around its body and the weight
of the pebbles brought it to the ground. This
method of capturing dragonflies in Japan
is known as *buri* or *toriko*. Reportedly, it
works, but with a success rate of somewhat
less than five percent.

Hadland Davis, in *Myths and Legends of
Japan*, described a somewhat easier method
of catching dragonflies. According to

Davis, some Japanese believe that if they
trace a certain ideograph in the air, it will
paralyze the dragonfly they wish to catch.
Actually, the idea is to mesmerize the
dragonfly by holding one of your hands out
in front of you and slowly, but methodi-
cally, moving it in some pattern (a figure eight
is a favorite) as you approach. Supposedly,
the dragonfly becomes so intent on your
hand that it fails to notice the rather
large person behind the hand poised to
grab it.

The Dragonfly in Chinese Folklore

As evidenced by recent excavations of dragonfly fossils from the fossil-rich Yixian
formation near Beipiao, China, the dragonfly has been a part of the insect fauna of
China for an extremely long time. These
fossilized dragonflies apparently differ little in overall size and shape from the so-
called *ching-t'ing* found in China today.

Ching-t'ing is the most commonly used
name for the dragonfly in China. *Ching*
means "greenish in color," and *t'ing* means
a "pointed thing," a "streak," or "like a
stick" *[Figure 14]*. The Chinese people make

references to the dragonfly in their everyday speech. The term *shu ching-t'ing* means "to stand on one's head" or "to do a headstand" and refers to the ability of the dragonfly to poise motionless in the air. In boxing, "dragonfly thrust" describes the motion of a boxer as he darts in close to his opponent, delivers a quick blow, and darts back out of range.

The dragonfly is sometimes called the "typhoon fly" because it is often present in large numbers before a storm. It is also known by the slang expression "old glassy" because of the clear, glasslike appearance of its wings. A colloquial term for the dragonfly in China is *ma-lang*. *Ma* is part of *macha* (locust) and *lang* is part of the appellation *t'ang-lang* (praying mantis), with which the dragonfly is often confused.

In *Folklore of the Dragonfly: A Linguistic Approach*, Eden E. Sarot quotes a song sung by the children of the Peiping (Beijing) area, which goes as follows:

Ma-lang, ma-lang kuo ho lai
His-fu, his-fu shai lo lai.
(Dragonfly, dragonfly, come and cross the river!
O daughter-in-law, come and sift the flour.)

Sarot also quotes an interesting children's song sung in colloquial Cantonese where the dragonfly is called *t'ong-me*.

"T'ong-me fi ko,
Ha u ch'o-ch'o."
(When the dragonflies fly high, there will be
a downpour of rain from the sky.)

Dragonflies appear in the writings of one of the greatest of the Chinese poets, Tu Fu (712–770), who dominated Chinese literature for almost ten centuries. He wrote of them in one of two poems translated as "Meandering River" in the book *Sunflower Splendor: Three Thousand years of Chinese Poetry* by Wu-Chi Liu and Irving Yucheng Lo (1975).

Deep among the flowers, butterflies
press their way;
The slow-winged dragonflies dot
the water.
I'd whisper to the wind and light:
"Together let's tarry;
We shall enjoy the moment, and never
contrary be."

The following poem from the same book, written by Liu Yu-hsi (772–842) during the Tang Dynasty, is one of the more evocative poems about a dragonfly. The story goes that a lady of means, with

{FIGURE 14}

Ching-t'ing, a common name used for the dragonfly in China, means a greenish, pointed, or stick-like thing, such as this female Great Pondhawk (Erythemis vesiculosa). *Photo © James L. Lasswell.*

her husband away from home, did not know what to do with herself, so she counted one by one the blossoms in her garden. As she was counting the blossoms, a dragonfly flew up and alighted on her jade hairpin. The actions of this dragonfly were thought to be very daring, for the lady was considered to be an aristocrat and no creature was supposed to approach anyone of her stature without permission.

"A Song of Spring"
Down she comes from her vermilion tower, her face freshly adorned.
Deeply immured spring light fills the courtyard with sadness.
She strolls to the center of the Garden to count blossoms,
As a dragonfly flies up and alights on her jade hairpin.

The Dragonfly in Filipino Folklore

In *Filipino Popular Tales* (1965), Dean S. Fansler relates an amusing folktale, shortened here, entitled "The Monkeys and the Dragonflies."

In this tale, a monkey drove a female dragonfly away from her perch, whereupon she told her brother (the king of the dragonflies). This made the king of the dragonflies angry, and he vowed to make war upon the monkeys. When it came time for the battle, the dragonflies arrived empty-handed while the monkeys were armed with clubs. The monkey-king ordered his soldiers to strike the flying creatures with their clubs. Hearing this, the king of the dragonflies commanded his soldiers to light upon the foreheads of the monkeys. The dragonflies would light upon the forehead of a monkey, and as another monkey tried to strike the dragonfly it would quickly dart away. The monkey on which the dragonfly had been perched was struck in the forehead with the club instead. The dragonflies were not hurt, but the monkeys were all killed. Thus the light, quick-witted dragonflies won the victory over the strong but foolish monkeys.

Over the centuries, people have become more enlightened about the aesthetic and beneficial qualities of dragonflies, but old fears and superstitions still persist. Our perceptions and beliefs about the creatures of nature are often influenced by other people. Eventually, perhaps the good things about dragonflies will replace the apprehensions and take their rightful place in the folklore passed from generation to generation.

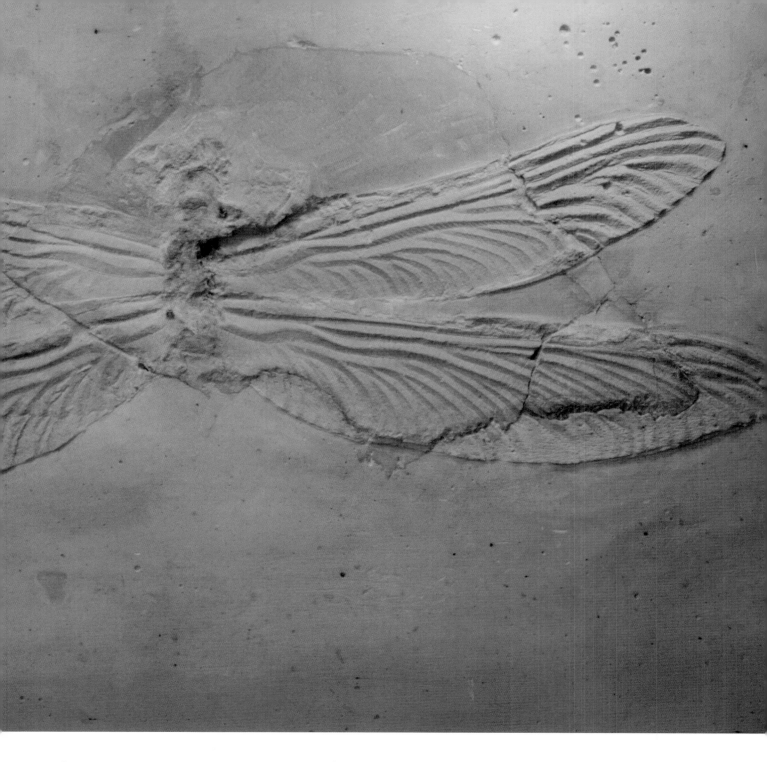

{ CHAPTER THREE }

THE PREHISTORY
OF DRAGONFLIES

Dragonflies arose many millions of years before the dinosaurs, and their lineage is one of the oldest among insects. Numerous groups and species have been preserved over the ages, and an abundant fossil record has allowed scientists to contemplate the phylogeny—the genetic relationships through time—and evolution of dragonflies for many years.

To separate the species and organize them into orders and families, scientists rely mainly on differences in wing venation, the spidery network of lines in their wings that give dragonflies part of their characteristic appearance. That most dragonflies can be identified based solely on their wings is fortunate because very often the wings are all that remain in a fossil. The few examples that include a preserved body are important because the older the fossil formation, the scarcer they become. The vein patterns are characteristic enough, however, that even fragments of preserved wings

{DETAIL}

See Figure 17 in full on page 47.

can place the fossil dragonfly into a genus or species. The wings can also be used to deduce the size of the dragonfly even if none of the body was preserved.

The Earliest Dragonflies

No one knows exactly how old dragonflies really are. The earliest known fossils of dragonfly-like insects, called eugeropterids after the family name Eugeropteridae, are from the Carboniferous period and are about 325 million years old. As far as we know, these were not excessively large insects, probably no bigger than modern dragonflies. But they were interesting in a number of ways, not the least of which was the presence of a third pair of reduced wings just over the front pair of legs *[Figure 15]*.

All modern insects possess only two pairs of wings over the second and third pairs of legs, and some groups, like the flies, have only one pair of developed wings. Referred to as "winglets," and considered a primitive feature in insects, the additional wings of the eugeropterids resemble the small airfoils in front of the wings of some fighter

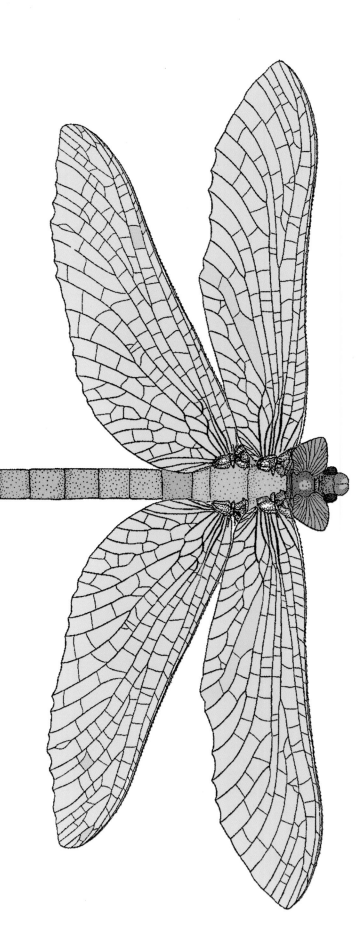

Reconstruction of an unidentified eugeropterid from Argentina showing the winglets near the head. The original fossil is approximately 325 million years old, the oldest known dragonfly-like insect. Figure courtesy of Dr. Jarmila Kukalova-Peck, Carleton University, Ottawa, Canada.

jets, which help add stability during high-speed flight. Not all aspects of the eugeropterids, however, were primitive. Their wings had already developed adaptations for flight similar to those of modern species. Because the evolved traits for flight are present in the oldest known dragonfly group, there are likely even older and more primitive dragonflies to be discovered in the fossil record. The lineage may be many millions of years older than we currently know.

We can determine that these ancient dragonflies were evolving control of their flight by comparing their wings with those of modern dragonflies. The wings of all dragonflies and their relatives have a characteristic set of veins that serve as spars and stays to support the wing in flight, without which the wing would be no more useful than cellophane flapping in a breeze. Imagine a kite without its supports—it could never catch the wind and stay aloft. In addition to these obvious structural support functions, the veins also impart a number of passive but important flight functions to the wing that contribute to the dragonfly's maneuverability.

Although they appear flat when observed from above, dragonfly wings are actually three dimensional. In a side view, along the plane of the wing, it is easy to see that the veins create ridges and valleys in the flat surface from wingtip to the body. These ripples change relative to one another as the wings flap, just as the feathers in a bird's wings constantly change positions when the bird flies. These positional changes, whether in a bird or a dragonfly, affect the physics of flight. As the veins shift, they form structures that provide more lift.

In modern dragonflies, one of these structures consists of the triangles of cells in the wing next to the body. By folding and changing shape with the downstroke, the triangles both support the wing and cause it to form a dynamic airfoil. During this stroke, where most of the power for flight would be expected, the trailing edge of the wing stiffens and curls down, an adaptation similar to the flaps on an airplane that provide not only extra lift, but also stability at low flight speeds. These triangles are absent in the ancient eugeropterids, but their function was replicated by a different set of veins that formed a quadrangle or parallelogram

{ F I G U R E 16 }

The abdomen of an unknown meganeurid showing the large ovipositor, or egg-laying organ, from the earliest Permian deposits in Hamilton, Kansas. Fossil courtesy of Dr. Chris Durden, Texas Memorial Museum, Austin, Texas. Photo by James L. Lasswell.

instead. The presence of these similar structures implies that the ancient insects were on a similar (though not the same) evolutionary path to the aerobatic flight capabilities achieved by the modern dragonflies. The advanced wing feature indicates that eugeropterids had been evolving well before their fossils were formed and that, even though no physical evidence of them has yet been found, older dragonfly fossils are surely waiting to be discovered.

Another ancient line of dragonflies is from the Permian period, which began approximately 300 million years ago and ended with the Triassic period some 250 million years before modern time. These are the giant dragonflies, referred to as meganeurids after the family name Meganeuridae. While they were very similar in shape to modern Odonata, the size of these creatures is what sets them apart [Figures 16, 17]. Some of the meganeurids were

This fossil of Tupus permianus *was found in Dickinson County, Kansas, in a barnyard at Elmo Well. Considered lost by Frank Carpenter in his 1939 paper on the lower Permian insects of Kansas, it is currently in the Texas Memorial Museum in Austin, Texas. Fossil courtesy of Dr. Chris Durden, Texas Memorial Museum, Austin, Texas. Photo by James L. Lasswell.*

the largest flying insects ever known. The fossilized forewing of *Meganeuropsis americana,* discovered in Noble County, Oklahoma, measures 280 millimeters (11.2 inches) and is estimated to have been 305 millimeters (12 inches) in total length. The wingspan would have been some 686 millimeters (27 inches). *Meganeuropsis permiana,* the largest fossil insect so far discovered was retrieved from the Elmo formations of Kansas. It had a wing length estimated at 330 millimeters (13 inches) with an approximate wingspan of 710 millimeters (28 inches).

These giant creatures are known mostly from fossilized wings because the bodies did not preserve well. Several remarkable specimens, however, have been found in the coal beds of Commentry, France, and provide insight into the body forms of these insects. Features such as long antennae and prognathous (forward projecting) mandibles reminiscent of beetles appear in the reconstructions. A fossil found at this location and originally identified as a primitive grasshopper may actually be a larva of one of these fantastic insects.

Another mark of distinction, besides size, that separates the meganeurids from other families of dragonflies is the relative simplicity of their wings. Although many of the modern veins are present and recognizable, there is little specialization such as that found in the eugeropterids or the modern Odonata, and this simple pattern changes little over their history. Since no wing structures enhanced flight, these giants would have been slower and less agile than their counterparts in other families.

The family Meganeuridae disappeared during the catastrophic Permian extinction, when most of the species on Earth were annihilated. Yet in their time, they were the rulers of the sky, since no larger flying creatures are known from this period.

The Mesozoic Era

The end of the Permian period also brought to a close the end of the Paleozoic era. The new era, the Mesozoic, is known mostly for the appearance of huge dinosaurs and other fantastic creatures that populated land, sea, and sky. Strata from the three major periods of this era all contain dragonfly fossils. While some exist from the Triassic period, the oldest of the Mesozoic periods, many modern families of dragonflies begin to appear in the Jurassic period.

One great fossil bed from this age has yielded some of the most finely detailed dragonfly remains ever found. The limestone bed in Solnhofen, near the Danube River in Bavaria, has produced such specimens as the famous *Archaeopteryx* fossil—the eerily reptilian bird once hailed as the missing link between birds and reptiles. About 150 million years ago, conditions were such that creatures buried here had much of their delicate and otherwise unknown detail preserved, especially in their bodies.

The Solnhofen region was a large, subtropical lagoon at the very end of the Jurassic, a time that evokes images of luxurious plant growth and teeming aquatic life. Yet this lagoon was normally filled with salt water so concentrated that very few organisms could survive in it. When an animal died and settled to the bottom, there were no scavengers to claim the carcass.

Cyanobacteria, so ancient that we are not sure if they are algae or bacteria, are one of the few organisms that can live in such hypersaline water, and they grew in a thick mat on the bottom sediment. This mat may also have been responsible, in part, for the level of detail preserved in these creatures. Scientists postulate that the mat grew quickly over the carcasses and protected them from the immediate ravages of oxidation and decay. Silt and mud then settled over the encased organism, protecting them even further.

Many Solnhofen fossils reside in collections and museums around the world. Their abundance is due to heavy mining in area quarries and the subsequent large amount of processed rock it produced. At least thirteen groups of Odonata have been recovered, and enough individual specimens have been found that they can be sold at rock and gem shows and in dealer galleries.

The Yixian formation near Beipiao in the Chinese province of Liaoning produces extremely detailed fossils. This site is a sedimentary deposit from the early Cretaceous period, which followed the

Jurassic and lasted from approximately 145 million years ago until the extinction of the dinosaurs 65 million years ago. Fabulous discoveries, including feathered dinosaurs, have been made at this site, and it has been described as the most important to be uncovered in the twentieth century.

Included among the ancient angiosperms and primitive birds are numerous dragonflies, both larvae and adults. So well preserved are these fossils that larvae can be associated with the adult form in the species *Aeschnidium heishankowense,* a member of the extinct family Aeschnidiidae—a widespread group throughout the ancient world that is commonly found in the Yixian deposits.

Because the fossils of *A. heishankowense* are so extensive, scientists have been able to speculate on the life history of the species. Even though it has been extinct for over 130 million years it probably lived in much the same way that dragonflies do today. The larvae had a sprawling form, adapted to burrow in the soft bottoms of the shallow lakes they inhabited. By hiding in the mud or sand on the lake bottom the larvae could ambush their prey, which included contemporary aquatic insects. The larvae were large enough that they may have taken small fish as well. In spite of a mostly sedentary lifestyle, they appeared to have been capable swimmers when the need arose. The adults were large, with wide wings adapted to move long distances, rather like modern-day dragonflies called saddlebags (genus *Tramea*) and gliders (genus *Pantala*). Since the fossils suggest that both their wings and bodies were brown, they may have fed at dusk when the darkening sky and shadows provided the best camouflage.

Another well-known site for the discovery of Cretaceous fossils is the Santana formation in Araripe, Brazil. Nearly 900 meters (3,000 feet) above sea level, the Araripe Plateau was for at least some period in its existence a shallow, nutrient-rich, freshwater lake in a somewhat arid climate. Specimens from this formation are over 100 million years old and conserved in carbon, which, in part, is why their detail is so well preserved. Known mostly for fish fossils, the Santana formation has also produced some remarkable dragonfly specimens as well. A large collection of fossils from this region has been placed in the American Museum of Natural History through the effort of

Herbert R. Axelrod, a leading figure in the tropical fish field.

Modern Thought

While prehistoric dragonflies are well represented in the fossil record, scientists do not always agree on how to categorize them. There are various interpretations of dragonfly origins, and the higher levels of classification, such as suborders and super-families, are currently in contention. Disagreement often centers on whether or not a particular feature of a dragonfly can be considered "primitive," that is, existed first, or "advanced," meaning derived from or beyond the primitive state. The designation primitive does not necessarily reflect on a feature's adaptive value at the time. Being a poor flier probably would not matter if nothing else could fly.

The conundrum arises when scientists try to determine the relationships of the various dragonfly species through time and apply the study of evolution to the issues of classification, or taxonomy. Wing veins and other physical features used by taxonomists to classify dragonflies underwent evolutionary changes, with new and different dragonfly species evolving away from common ancestors and from each other. Many of these species simply died out. Lineages now extinct may have been very successful in the period in which they lived, but their successful adaptations usually radiate away into dead ends that hide and confuse the true trail. Not enough fossils have been found to yield a sufficient record and allow an objective tracking of dragonfly parentage and ancestry.

Reconstructing a prehistoric phylogeny, or genetic line, and relating it to living species is much like reconstructing a puzzle with many or most of the pieces missing. Paleontologists must use the best evidence available and then bridge the gaps with theories and insights until new evidence or a consensus of interpretation emerges. More work needs to be done and more fossils discovered before scientists will agree upon the details of the evolution of dragonflies.

The classification of living, along with extinct, dragonflies is not without debate. Most entomologists currently acknowledge two suborders of Odonata, the Zygoptera, or damselflies, and the Anisoptera, or dragonflies. Many authorities, however, also recognize a third suborder, the Anisozygoptera. Members of this suborder were abundant in the Mesozoic period, but, some argue, perished with the dinosaurs. Two living representatives of the group may still exist. These are *Epiophlebia superstes* [see Figure 11] found in Japan and elsewhere in Asia, and *Epiophlebia laidlawi*, a Himalayan species. These unusual insects have both dragonfly and damselfly characteristics, along with some features unique to themselves, and are probably the oldest living lineage of Odonata. In spite of the fact that they have been scientifically described and studied since 1889 and 1921 respectively, there is no firm consensus as to how to classify them.

The discovery of more fossil beds that provide reasonably good dragonfly specimens would contribute greatly to filling the gaps in dragonfly phylogeny and erasing current confusion. While no fossils of any winged insects are currently available that significantly predate the oldest eugeropterids, scientists believe they are there, waiting in their stone tombs until by chance a pair of trained eyes happens to look in just the right place.

New Technology—Old Problems

Two of the most far-reaching developments of the twentieth century have been information technology (IT) and molecular biology. One might think that molecular and gene technologies would have a greater impact on the study of dragonflies than IT would. Yet digital scanning technology allowed the creation of the Digital Dragonflies site on the World Wide Web, which led to the writing of this book. Quality websites on Odonata are increasing, and the ability of researchers and enthusiasts around the world to reach one another has dramatically helped fuel interest in these insects.

How do the advances of molecular biology affect the study of dragonflies? In spite of high expectations, not as much as anticipated. Many entomological studies that involve this approach focus on economically important insects. Pests such as mosquitoes, aphids, and caterpillars or useful insects, such as honeybees, receive the most attention from molecular biologists. The majority of their work concentrates on insects as biological models for medical or genetic research. The fruit fly, *Drosophila melanogaster,* was the first insect to have its entire genome sequenced and has been a prime model for genetic studies for decades.

The Odonata cannot claim any of these distinctions. Intractable in the laboratory and innocuous in the field, the dragonfly's claim on our attention is largely aesthetic. This is not to say the group has been entirely ignored. As of this writing, there are 934 dragonfly DNA sequences currently kept in GenBank—the huge online repository. For comparison, there are 345,141 representing the Lepidoptera (moths and butterflies) and 1,106,640 relating to the Diptera (flies), the bulk of which involve the above-mentioned *Drosophila* and *Anopheles gambiae* (the malaria mosquito).

Of what use is DNA sequence information? Like the physical features on a dragonfly, such as wing veins, DNA sequences can be compared with one another to estimate the degree of relatedness between species, genera, and families. In one sense, looking directly at DNA may offer the ultimate solution to the nagging and contentious problems confronting scientists who are trying to unravel the history of these ancient creatures. The actual sequence of the DNA that comprises genes (unlike the physical features they regulate, which may be affected by environmental factors or suppressed by other genes) should provide exact information on how closely one dragonfly is related to another.

For living dragonflies, this is largely true. It is also true for the placement of dragonflies into a modern family tree representing the known orders of insects. In both instances, however, the conclusions of molecular biology support assessments already reached using less esoteric means.

Yet the question of dragonfly origins still remains a mystery. Under certain circumstances, DNA is a very stable molecule, but even it cannot last the hundreds of millions of years needed for us to examine the DNA of ancient dragonflies. The best we can do is to look at the DNA of modern descendants and try to reconstruct the ancient roadmap, a task that is not easy because so little is known about insect genes and genes in general.

DRAGONFLY LIVES

Insects are among the most common creatures on Earth. Students of biology and natural history are bombarded with astronomical estimates of the numbers of insect species populating the planet, perhaps over a million. In order to tally these numbers, scientists currently rely on a system of classification called the Linnaean system, first developed in the 1700s by Carl von Linné. Each life form is placed into groups, from large to ever-smaller ones, until it is by itself as a single species. While confusing to many people, the system allows taxonomists, scientists who deal with the classification of life, to sort, classify, and make useful inferences about all types of organisms.

Even more confusing, the organization and classification of life forms are under continual refinement as new insights come from researchers who constantly add to or change the information. Although these changes annoy students and others who use the taxonomy, or classification system, for purposes such as life lists or checklists, it is nonetheless important to have a flexible system that can account for new information and adapt accordingly.

Dragonflies Are Insects

In the Linnaean system, insects as a whole are categorized in a group called a class, derived from a larger group, the Phylum Arthropoda. Arthropods are characterized by the presence of an exoskeleton, a segmented body, and jointed appendages. Insects belong to Class Insecta, also referred to as Class Hexapoda. Insects have all the general features of arthropods but can be further characterized by the presence of three distinct body segments: the head, thorax, and abdomen. The head has one pair of antennae while the thorax has six legs, one pair for each of its own three segments. The abdomen has no true legs and may have as many as ten or eleven segments. The class category is organized into orders, where the insects appear in recognizable groups.

{FIGURE 18}

This dragonfly with the common name Flame Skimmer has been assigned the scientific designation Libellula saturata, *a name recognized by scientists worldwide. Photo © Greg W. Lasley.*

Here, in the Order Odonata, dragonflies begin to take on their distinct identity from other insects.

The next major taxonomic category sorts the orders even further, into families. Families are then broken down into other categories such as subfamily and tribe before arriving at the genus level. A genus name is the first part of the scientific name of a species. For example, the species name for humans is *Homo sapiens.* The genus is *Homo* while the specific name is *sapiens.* Together, the genus and specific name (also called the specific epithet) make up a scientific name. Here is an example of how the Flame Skimmer dragonfly *[Figure 18]* might be characterized under the Linnaean system:

Phylum: Arthropoda

Class: Insecta (*or* Hexapoda)

Order: Odonata

Family: Libellulidae

Genus: *Libellula*

Specific Epithet: *saturata*

By convention, genus and species names are normally italicized or underlined, while higher levels are not.

The Odonata, which includes the suborders Anisoptera (dragonflies) and Zygoptera (damselflies) [see Figure 3], is a small group as insect orders go. Of the 23 or so orders of insects currently recognized, the Odonata account for less than 7,000 species. The largest order, the Coleoptera or beetle family, has hundreds of thousands of species. But when compared with non-insect groups, the number of Odonata species assumes a different perspective. For instance, there are only about 9,000 known species of birds living today, just over 5,500 amphibian species, and less than 5,000 mammals. Yet the number of mammalogists, those who study mammals, herpetologists, those who study amphibians and reptiles, and ornithologists, those who study birds, far exceeds the number of odonatologists, those who study dragonflies and damselflies.

Our knowledge of dragonfly taxonomy begins with understanding both dragonfly development and morphology (form and structure). Dragonflies have two very separate phases of their lives, the larva (also known as nymph or naiad) or immature phase and the adult or winged reproductive

{FIGURE 19}

A female Neon Skimmer (Libellula croceipennis) *laying eggs while being guarded by a male of the same species. Photo © Curtis E. Williams.*

phase. In these two phases, they do not resemble one another, a common occurrence in many groups of insects. The transformation from immature insects to adults can be gradual—true bugs change a little more with each molt to resemble the adult. Or it can be extreme, such as with some flies, which change from the immature shapeless, legless lump of a maggot to an adult fly through a pupal, or intermediate, stage.

Since dragonfly adults and larvae do not resemble each other, a scientific key to relevant characteristics used to identify one will not work for the other. Like butterflies and their corresponding caterpillars, each has very specialized features.

The Immature Stages

The first stage of dragonfly life is the egg, which is deposited by the female in a variety of locations. In the simplest case, the female dips the tip of her abdomen in the water and the eggs wash away to their individual fates. This is a familiar sight over ponds, since it is the normal means used by a group of abundant and familiar dragonflies common to still water, the skimmers. There are, however, some elaborations. The female Neon Skimmer (*Libellula croceipennis*) flips her eggs away from her as she dips her abdomen into the water [Figure 19]. Small fish attracted to the splashing miss the sinking eggs, which in turn avoid becoming fish food.

Other dragonflies, notably the darners, have saw-like ovipositors, or egg-laying organs. Developed appendages on the ends of their abdomens dig into plant stems or even dead wood. The female injects the eggs into the selected location, where they are more protected than those laid in the open. This method is also fairly easy to observe due to the widespread distribution of a species that uses it, the Common Green Darner (*Anax junius*). Females, usually with the male attached, will crawl in or on vegetation or dead plant material floating in the water. They may partially submerge themselves as they probe with the tip of their abdomen searching for acceptable spots to lay their eggs [Figure 20]. These and other species may also lay eggs on or in soil or mud. The female spiketails (family Cordulegastridae) are prime examples; they drive their ovipositors into submerged soil sediments to lay eggs [Figure 21].

The duration of the egg stage varies and depends on many circumstances. The eggs are very small, and while the eggs of some species can hatch in less than a week, others may take months. Cooler temperatures are a predominant factor and can delay hatch time, both by slowing development and, depending on the dragonfly species, by putting eggs into diapause, a sort of hibernation that delays hatching mainly for the purpose of surviving over a winter.

Once eggs hatch, the larvae begin the mobile stages of their lives. The first stage after hatch, the prolarva, normally goes unnoticed because of its short duration, perhaps less than a minute [Figure 22]. This cryptic stage appears to be a survival

{FIGURE 20}

A female Common Green Darner (Anax junius) *laying eggs while in tandem with a male. Photo © Curtis E. Williams.*

mechanism that allows the larva to reach water if it needs to before its first molt into an aquatic larva. If an egg has been laid in the upper parts of plants, or if water has receded from where the egg was placed, the hatchling may find itself in a dry environment. Still enclosed in embryonic membranes with no appendages yet free, the prolarva must thrash or flip until it finds water. If the egg is already in water or the prolarva is successful in reaching water, the first molt into the second larval stage, also referred to as the second stadium, proceeds *[Figure 23]*. The larva has now begun its life as a predator, and even though it is almost microscopic, its basic body plan will remain until it emerges as an adult dragonfly.

Dragonflies and all other insects have an external skeleton, or exoskeleton. They are

unable to grow unless they shed the old exoskeleton and make a new one. The number of times this shedding, or molt, occurs varies among different dragonfly species, but normally they molt ten to fifteen times, with twelve being average. The number fluctuates even within a species—additional molts may occur if the larva is exposed to adverse temperatures, an unfavorable environment, or other unusual circumstances.

Raising a dragonfly from egg to adult in order to count its larval stadia is a difficult enterprise. Phillip Corbet of the University of Edinburgh collected data on molting, and in his 1996 publication reported information for only 83 species, including damselflies. Scientists have generally found it easier to count backward from the last stage of a larva's life—the one before its final molt to a free-flying adult. While very young larvae are difficult to see, larvae large enough to capture and observe in an aquarium can have their molts easily recorded. Once the final molt occurs, then the previous life stages may be assigned numbers. For instance, a larva that molts three times before the final molt to adult was captured at the F-3 stage or four stadia before adult. After the first molt, it became F-2, after the second molt, it became F-1, after the third molt it became F-0, after which the final molt to the adult stage occurred. If we happen to know that this particular species has twelve larval stages (counting the prolarval stage), then it was captured in the eighth stadium.

The advantage of counting backward from the last larval stage is that it allows a large degree of standardization in describing immature stages within a dragonfly species. No matter how many molts a larva of any species makes, there is no difficulty in determining which one is the last one and counting the number of molts it has made while in captivity.

The dragonfly larva is typical of the larvae of most insects in that it has three main body

{FIGURE 22}

*Eggs and prolarva
(first stage after
hatch) of the Jade
Clubtail* (Arigomphus
submedianus). *Photo
© Curtis E. Williams.*

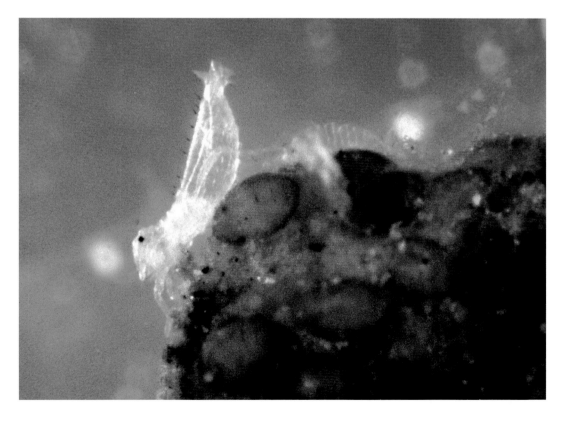

{FIGURE 23}

*Eggs and the second
stadium (first stage
after prolarva)
nymph of the Jade
Clubtail* (Arigomphus
submedianus). *Photo
© Curtis E. Williams.*

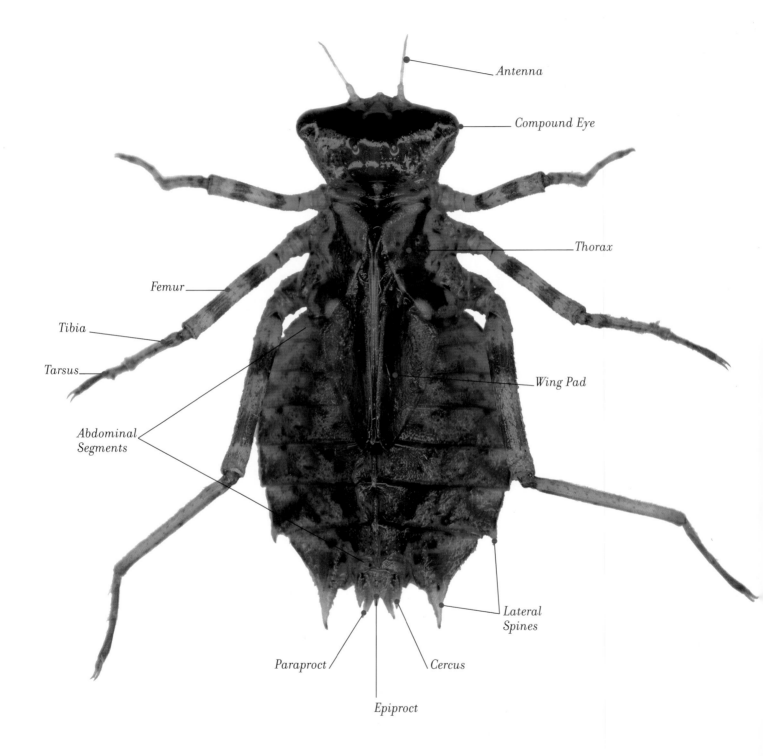

Larva of the Prince Baskettail
(Epitheca princeps), *labeled to show*
parts of the body. Scan provided by
authors.

Antenna

Compound Eye

Thorax

Femur

Tibia

Tarsus

Wing Pad

Abdominal
Segments

Lateral
Spines

Paraproct

Cercus

Epiproct

regions, the head, thorax, and abdomen [Figure 24]. On the head are the antennae, eyes, and mouthparts. The antennae are short, a feature shared by many aquatic insects, although unlike other insects dragonfly antennae have few specialized sensory organs. Some species may use the antennae in a tactile role to detect prey in circumstances where vision is either non-functional or impaired.

The eyes are compound, that is, they are made up of numerous individual single eyes or simple eyes called ommatidia. Each ommatidium is supplied with a nerve connection and able to see, but all function together as a unit, forming a composite image that provides the excellent vision characterizing these insects. The shape of the eye varies from species to species. In some the eye is little more than a protuberance jutting from the head; in others it is almost as well developed as the eye of the adult. A darner in its last larval stage, for example, has up to 8,000 ommatidia. The number of ommatidia composing the eye and the character of each individual ommatidium changes throughout the life of a larva. At each molt the larva

grows and adds new ommatidia. The function of old ommatidia may change—one that looked forward may well end up looking rearward by the final stage.

Dragonflies are carnivorous in all larval stages and as adults. The larvae locate their prey using their excellent vision, but that is only half the job. Once found, the intended victim must be captured. The arrangement of the mouthparts and the unique adaptations of the larvae represent a remarkable feature of dragonflies and work in harmony with their acute vision to catch food.

The rearmost segment of the mouthparts, the labium, has developed into a hinged apparatus that quickly extends, grabs the prey, and retracts, bringing the prey to the mandibles, which then rend it into pieces small enough to swallow [Figure 25]. All Odonata larvae have this feature, but there are slight modifications from species to species, differences pronounced enough to use for identification. The labium itself is divided into two main sections, the prementum and the postmentum (or the mentum and the submentum), which have a hinge between them. There is also a hinge

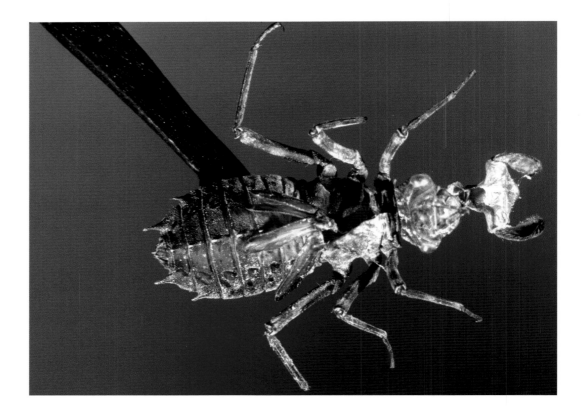

Exuvia, or larval shell, of the Orange Shadowdragon (Neurocordulia xanthasoma) *showing extended labium, the mouthpart that grabs prey (on right). The remains of the wing pads, attached to the thorax, are also visible. Photo © Curtis E. Williams.*

at the base of the postmentum where it attaches beneath the head. On the end of the prementum are two specialized lobes, known as palps, armed with teeth and bristle-like setae—specialized hairs produced by certain epidermal cells.

Scientists who study the labium have arrived at an accurate assessment of how it works. Speed in extending the labium is essential in snaring prey and is accomplished by hydraulics. Along with an external skeleton, insects, including dragonflies, have an open circulatory system, meaning there are no vessels, such as veins and capillaries, that enclose blood. In very simplistic terms, insects are an outer tube, the exoskeleton, surrounding an inner tube, the intestinal tract. Muscles attach from various points on the internal portions of the exoskeleton, rather like scaffolding, and organs are placed throughout the body so that the space between the gut and exoskeleton (the hemocoel) is far from empty. Even so, there is room for the blood, or hemolymph, to flow anywhere in the body from anywhere else. If one end of the body is squeezed, the hemolymph is forced into the other end.

In the case of a dragonfly larva, a set of muscles in the abdomen, referred to as a diaphragm, contracts and forces hemolymph into the head. Muscles in the labium briefly resist the hydraulic pressure, allowing force to build, and then release, causing the assembly to snap forward at high speed. The hook-like teeth on the palps, which actually snare the prey, are thrown open while forward momentum exists. On contact with the prey, forward motion slows or stops and the palps close. The teeth and setae now grapple the victim, and muscular action retracts it back to the mouth, where the mandibles begin their job.

The body sections behind the head and in front of the abdomen are collectively called the thorax, which is subdivided into three sections containing the six walking legs and the wings. Each section of the thorax bears a pair of legs and each of the last two sections has a pair of wing pads. During the larval stage the wings are developing and may be hard to see in younger larvae. Even in the last stadium before molting to an adult they are only pads and are non-functional. The size of the wing pads is an indicator of the age of the larva—the longer the pads, the older the larva. Within a species, detailed study and careful measurement of the pads can help determine the life stage of the larva and when it will emerge as an adult. In older larvae that have been hiding on the bottom of a pond, the wing pads may gather organisms such as algae, midge larvae, or nematodes that house themselves in the folds of the wing cover. They do not appear to harm the larva and are shed along with the skin at the next molt.

The legs of dragonfly larvae attach to the sides of their thoraxes. Although not as highly specialized as in some insects, adaptations on some species facilitate burrowing in sediment, tactile reception, and to a degree swimming. Legs consist of the coxa, a swiveling joint that connects the leg to the body, the trochanter, a short section between the coxa and the next section, the femur. The femur is the first long section of the leg, followed by the tibia or second long section, and finally the segmented tarsus or tip section containing the pretarsus and tarsal claws. Short spines may appear on the femur and tibia, but this varies by species.

The larva's abdomen is divided into ten segments and does not have any legs, although it has other major specializations. Dragonfly larvae are truly aquatic, that is, they breathe in and acquire oxygen from the water in which they live. There are a few exceptions to this, and many, if not most, larvae can live for long periods out of water or without being completely submerged. But in order to successfully develop to the adult stage, larvae require water.

Dragonflies were originally thought to have a passive respiratory system because they do not have lungs, which actively move air in and out, but rather a system of tubes called trachea that carries oxygen throughout the body. In terrestrial insects and adult dragonflies, the openings of these tubes to the outside atmosphere are called spiracles. As the trachea extend inward from these openings, they branch and become smaller tubes, called tracheoles, which are usually filled with liquid. Atmospheric oxygen dissolves into the liquid and then migrates across the tracheoles into the blood. Blood cells, or hemocytes, acquire the oxygen and then move it to the various tissues and organs in the body. Unlike mammals, the part of the blood cell that acquires oxygen molecules is copper, not iron, which is why most insect blood is bluish-green instead of red.

In larvae, respiration is accomplished by a dense network of tracheoles lining the rectum, which itself is enlarged and full of water. Oxygen dissolves directly from the water into this network without first having to go through the larger sections of trachea. In order to prevent oxygen depletion in the water that bathes the rectal cavity, different muscles in the abdomen are used to expand and contract the rectum, moving fresh oxygenated water in and stale water out.

In an interesting study published in the January 24, 2003, issue of the journal

Science, Mark Westneat and his colleagues demonstrated that a number of insects in a variety of orders, including adult dragonflies, in fact have an active respiratory system. The large sections of trachea that are near the spiracles actually expand and contract, moving atmospheric gases and oxygen through the insect body in a manner very similar to lungs. We lack details of how dragonflies accomplish this, and we do not know whether a similar function occurs in larvae. But the fact that it happens in dragonflies, which have a long history of evolution, would indicate that it is not a recent development.

Another special adaptation of dragonfly larvae prevents fecal material from contaminating the rectal cavity and fouling the oxygen exchange surfaces. As food passes through the intestinal tract and becomes digested, it is encased in a membrane derived from the gut surface and formed into a pellet. This pellet is ejected, sometimes quite forcefully, from the rectum and away from the larva.

The anal opening to the rectum is through the tenth abdominal segment and is constricted. When the dragonfly larva wants to move quickly or suspend itself in the water, it can, by contracting the abdomen, force water from the rectum through the anal opening and jet propel itself through the water, rather like a squid or octopus. Because this sudden contraction could cause the mouthparts to shoot out, a muscle mechanism restricts the labium and locks it in place. Conversely, when the larva attacks prey, a constricting mechanism seals the opening of the rectum and prevents the release of a jet of water. Otherwise the larva would launch itself through the water at a time when it needs stealth and a steady aim to capture its meal. Jet propulsion is a special feature of dragonfly larvae that is not present in damselflies, which must swim by a writhing motion of the gill lamellae, the feathery external gills on the end of the abdomen.

Although eons old, the transformation of the aquatic larva to the aerial adult is still a marvel of biology. This process is called metamorphosis and occurs during the larval stages, leading to the final molt, when the adult emerges. Metamorphosis may proceed over a fairly long period of time, such as over a winter. Many of the events

{FIGURE 30}

The teneral Dusky Clubtail, with its wings and abdomen almost fully extended. Its wings are still folded over its back. Photo © Dave Westover.

{FIGURE 31}

The adult Dusky Clubtail with its wings and abdomen fully expanded. It is very fragile at this point and must rest while the veins and body harden to the rigidity needed for flight. Photo © Dave Westover.

are subtle and can only be seen in experimental procedures or by detailed observation. While these are invisible to the casual observer, their culmination in the final molt is not. This molt is a very critical time in the life of a dragonfly, a time at which it is defenseless against predators or foul weather. Like the birth of a child, once the process starts, it becomes inevitable, leaving the dragonfly at the mercy of fortune.

When emergence first begins, the dragonfly ceases feeding and must find a relatively safe spot from which to crawl out of the water. To an extent, dragonflies appear to be able to choose the time of actual

emergence, since they may cease to feed for several days before becoming an adult. They may also leave the water some time before the last molt begins. Some species prefer to climb up on twigs or vegetation that jut above the water, or on mats of algae floating on the water. Others may crawl onto the shore or on rocks, sometimes even up the trunks of nearby trees. In circumstances of drought when water levels are very low, the larvae may have no choice but to simply crawl up the bank as far as they can go. This has had consequences in the southern United States where the red imported fire ant (*Solenopsis invicta*) has

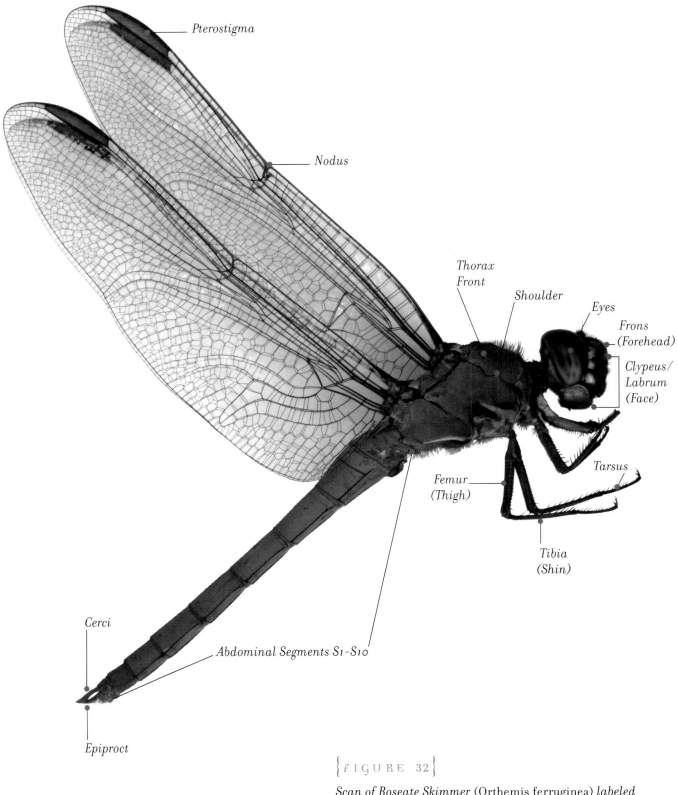

Pterostigma

Nodus

Thorax
Front

Shoulder

Eyes

Frons
(Forehead)

Clypeus/
Labrum
(Face)

Tarsus

Femur
(Thigh)

Tibia
(Shin)

Cerci

Abdominal Segments S1-S10

Epiproct

{FIGURE 32}

Scan of Roseate Skimmer (Orthemis ferruginea) labeled
to show parts of body. Scan provided by authors.

invaded the shores around water sources. Ants swarm the banks of lakes, streams, and ponds and aggressively attack any dragonflies that are attempting their final molt. The ants are also active at night, when this process normally occurs.

If the larva successfully finds a safe location away from the water, its legs stiffen and lock to the surface it is resting on. Then emergence begins [Figures 26-31]. The larva's skin starts to split along the top of the thorax. The back of the head capsule may also begin to break open. The adult pushes up and out of the skin, sometimes falling backward toward the water. The abdomen remains encased in the larval skin, serving as an anchor. As the adult legs pull free, the empty skin hardens and the legs act as clamps to hold the emerging dragonfly in place. The adult flops forward and its legs help pull the abdomen from the skin.

Once free of the larval shell, or exuvia, the adult does not really resemble a mature dragonfly. The abdomen is telescoped in, the wings are tiny, and the body is soft and shiny. Only the eyes give a hint of what is to come. The body begins to contract and the hemolymph is pumped into the wing veins. The veins and wings are as pliable and delicate as thin tissue. As the hemolymph fills the veins, the wings expand. Slowly they inflate, still translucent as opposed to transparent, a characteristic of teneral (freshly emerged) adults. Once the wings are full-size, the veins and vessels begin to harden in order to serve their next role as supports for the wing in flight. The dragonfly drains the hemolymph from its wings and starts to inflate its abdomen.

Instead of a series of veins, as in the wings, the abdomen is a hollow tube that is inflated. It is also soft at this time, since the hardening of the outer cuticle has not completed. Now at its full size, the dragonfly rests, its wing veins and body drying into the hard shells that will give it the rigidity needed for flight. This may take several hours.

The dragonfly can fly shortly after full inflation occurs, but it is a fluttering, inefficient flight that allows escape mostly from earthbound predators. The dragonfly is prone to damage if it flies before drying. If all goes well, it will be ready to take wing during the following day. It is not unusual to walk by the edge of a pond in the morning and have one or two teneral dragonflies flutter up from the surrounding vegetation and fly away. They are not as good at flying as they will become after several hours of drying, but within a day or so their aerobatic abilities are fully developed.

The Adult Stage

While the adult dragonfly has many typical insect qualities, it also has specialized features that support its way of life *[Figure 32]*. The head may be almost entirely covered by the compound eyes, much larger than those of the larva, which in turn are composed of different sizes of ommatidia that yield different resolutions of vision.

A striking feature of dragonfly eyes is the pseudopupils, dark points within the eye that move as the head turns, seemingly following the viewer *[Figures 33, 34]*. These are actually points of focus that are created by the size, shape, and orientation of the ommatidia. A number of the pseudopupils may be visible at once, and dragonflies can, in fact, see with all of them simultaneously, a trait that can be appreciated by anyone who has tried to sneak up on them.

Clusters of different-sized ommatidia can create bands, called foveal bands, across the eyes. The bands have different resolutions and purposes, and consequently the shape and focus of the pseudopupils within the bands can also change. Foveal bands may occur in different regions of the eye and be colored separately, as in the male Swamp Darner (*Epiaeschna heros*) *[Figure 35]*. A map of ommatidia sizes and viewing directions on the eye resembles a topographical map with very detailed lines of demarcation. An actual count in an adult Common Green Darner yielded 29,247 ommatidia making up the eye. Of these, 28,672 could be mapped to the pseudopupils.

The unusual mouthparts of the larva are now gone, replaced with a chewing mechanism typical to many insects. The mandibles are quite strong, as befits a predator, but not so strong as to constitute any danger to people or larger animals. There is one record in the scientific literature of a large unidentified dragonfly capturing and killing a Ruby-throated Hummingbird, but this is a remarkable and isolated event. A small hummingbird can weigh about two grams, easily within the power of the larger darners to lift, and if weakened after a migratory flight (and flying erratically enough to attract a dragonfly's attention) might well fall victim to an attack.

The adult antennae remain small, hair-like projections that have even less use than in the larval stage of life. In many species of insects, the antennae are heavily equipped with sensoria to identify food, sites for laying eggs, mates, and other benefits or dangers in their environment. These do not appear on the almost vestigial antennae of dragonflies, leading to the conclusion that they have little bearing on adult survival. Manipulations of adults in experiments reported no effect on these insects when the antennae were removed. Behavior and prey capture proceeded normally.

Although still bearing just the wings and legs, the three-segmented thorax of the adult is very different from the larval stage. The first

segment, just behind the head, is the smallest as it bears only the first pair of legs. The remaining two segments, however, bear not only legs but also the wings and are prominently enlarged to contain all the muscles needed to power the wings during flight.

The legs have now moved under the body rather than being arranged laterally as in the larva. None of the segments have been lost, but they are no longer used for walking. Instead, the legs are used to perch on vegetation, rocks, or the ground. Many species retract the front legs when they are at rest. Curiously, this pair of legs is pulled up and behind the head, almost in a striking position. It may be that they are simply in the way when grasping a twig. In photos of perched dragonflies, it is common to see some of the legs not contributing to the grip. Sometimes this is because the dragonfly has been posed after anesthesia, but even when not, legs may be astray.

{ FIGURE 33 }

Face of the Royal River Cruiser (Macromia taeniolata) *showing dark spots in the eyes called pseudopupils. The largest cruiser species in the United States, it lives primarily in the east and southeast. Photo © Curtis E. Williams.*

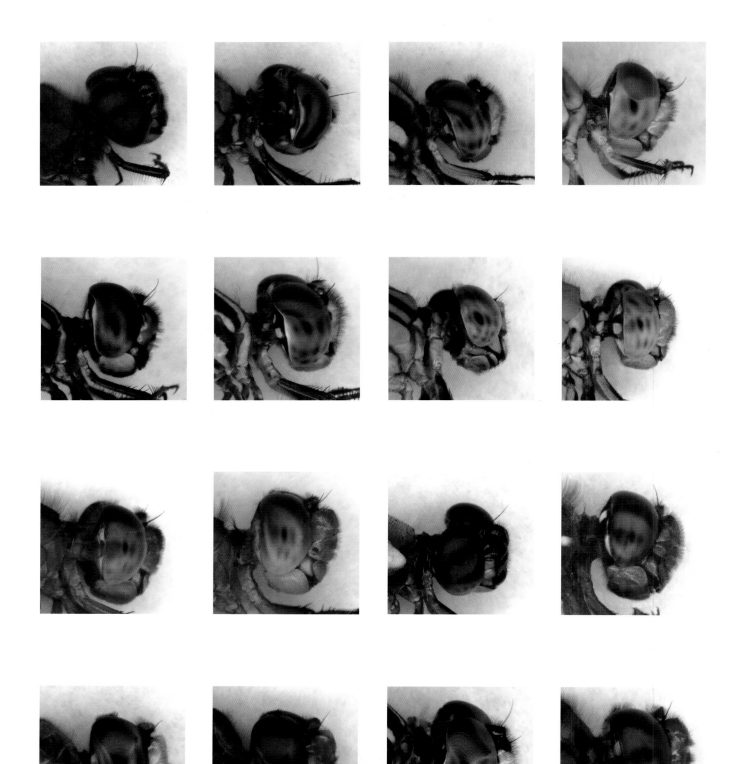

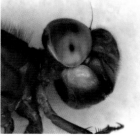

{FIGURE 34}

A collage of side scans of the heads of 30 different dragon-fly species. Note the differences in size and placement of the pseudopupils. Scans provided by authors.

{FIGURE 35}

Top view of a male Swamp Darner (Epiaeschna heros). *Note the placement of pseudopupils in the blue foveal band of its compound eyes. This species is found in the eastern and southeastern United States. Scan provided by authors.*

{FIGURE 36}

Scan of the wings of a Roseate Skimmer (Orthemis ferruginea) *labeled to show cells and veins of wings (terminology from Needham and Westfall 1955). Scan provided by authors.*

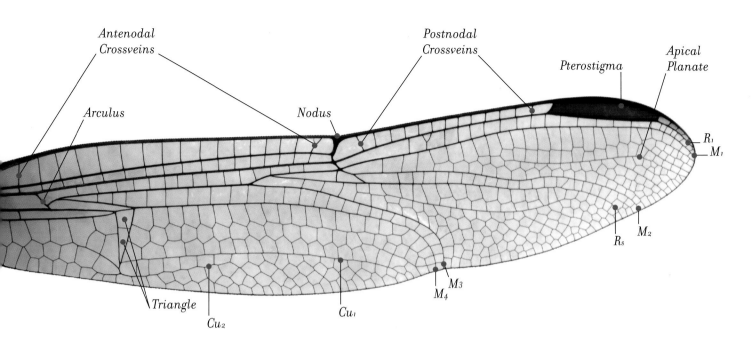

Antenodal
Crossveins

Arculus

Nodus

Postnodal
Crossveins

Pterostigma

Apical
Planate

R_1

M_1

R_s

M_2

M_3

M_4

Cu_1

Cu_2

Triangle

{FORE WING - ORTHEMIS FERRUGINEA}

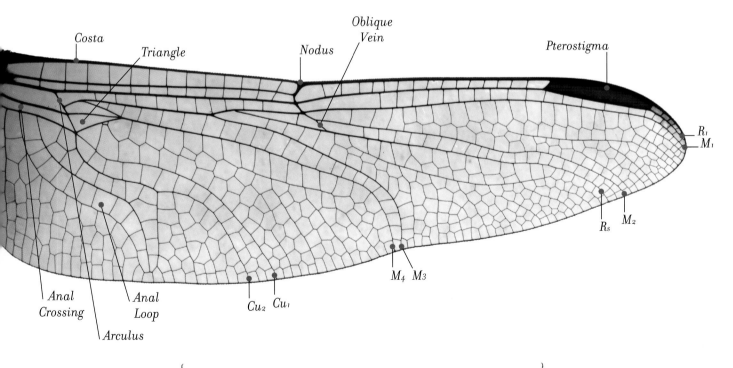

Costa

Triangle

Nodus

Oblique
Vein

Pterostigma

R_1

M_1

R_s

M_2

M_3

M_4

Cu_1

Cu_2

Anal
Crossing

Anal
Loop

Arculus

{HIND WING - ORTHEMIS FERRUGINEA}

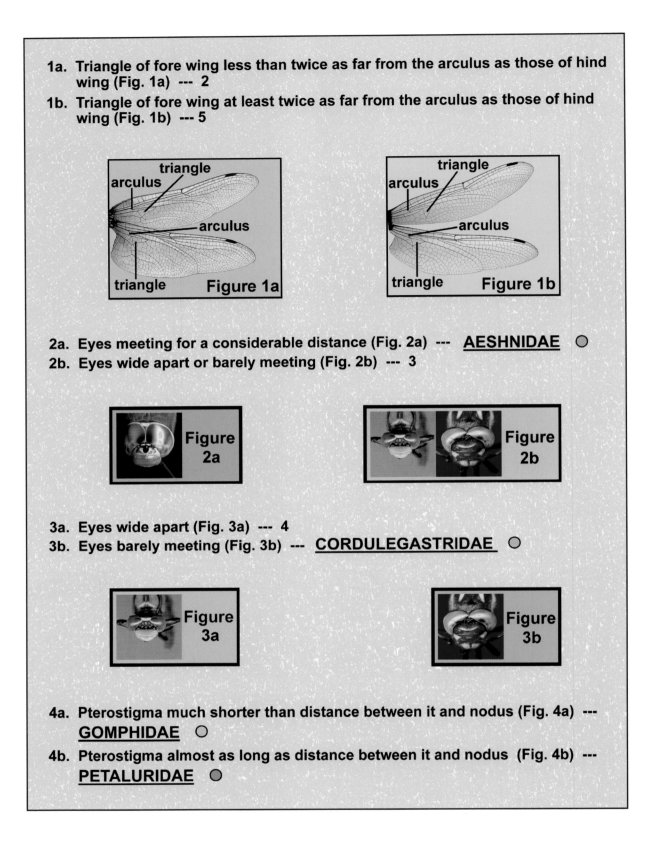

1a. Triangle of fore wing less than twice as far from the arculus as those of hind wing (Fig. 1a) --- 2

1b. Triangle of fore wing at least twice as far from the arculus as those of hind wing (Fig. 1b) --- 5

2a. Eyes meeting for a considerable distance (Fig. 2a) --- **AESHNIDAE** ○

2b. Eyes wide apart or barely meeting (Fig. 2b) --- 3

3a. Eyes wide apart (Fig. 3a) --- 4

3b. Eyes barely meeting (Fig. 3b) --- **CORDULEGASTRIDAE** ○

4a. Pterostigma much shorter than distance between it and nodus (Fig. 4a) --- **GOMPHIDAE** ○

4b. Pterostigma almost as long as distance between it and nodus (Fig. 4b) --- **PETALURIDAE** ○

{ f I G U R E 37 }

Page one of a pictorial key to the dragonfly families of North America. Image provided by authors.

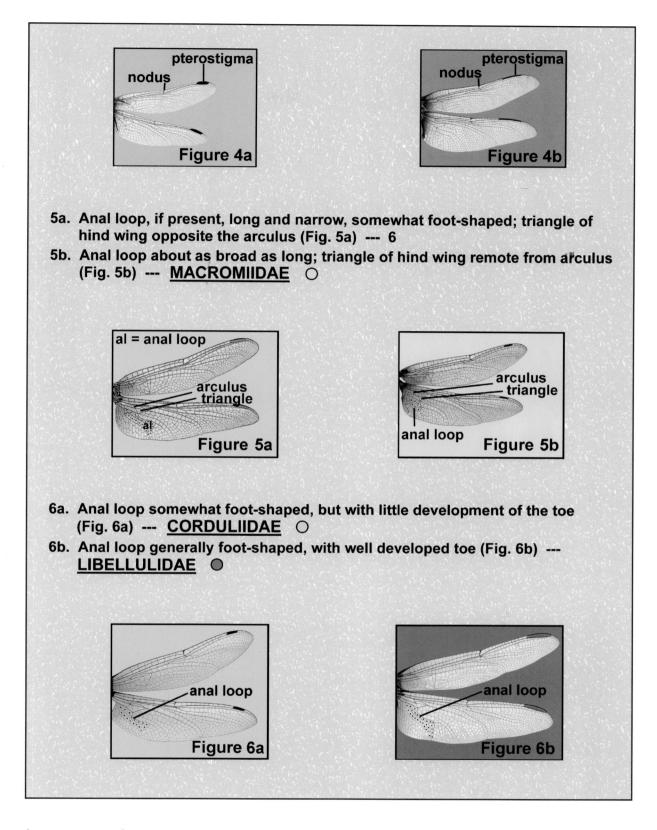

5a. Anal loop, if present, long and narrow, somewhat foot-shaped; triangle of hind wing opposite the arculus (Fig. 5a) --- **6**

5b. Anal loop about as broad as long; triangle of hind wing remote from arculus (Fig. 5b) --- <u>MACROMIIDAE</u> ○

6a. Anal loop somewhat foot-shaped, but with little development of the toe (Fig. 6a) --- <u>CORDULIIDAE</u> ○

6b. Anal loop generally foot-shaped, with well developed toe (Fig. 6b) --- <u>LIBELLULIDAE</u> ●

{ F I G U R E 38 }

Page two of a pictorial key to the dragonfly families of North America. Image provided by authors.

{FIGURE 39}

A collage of the abdomens of several different clubtail species (family Gomphidae) showing differences in terminal appendages. The tails (abdomens) were digitally removed from the scanned images of live dragonflies. Scans provided by authors.

In flight, the legs compose a basket underneath the dragonfly's body. As an aerial predator, it must catch its prey on the wing, which is accomplished by using the basket. Captured prey are passed up through the legs to the mouth and eaten either in flight or at rest. This essential feature of most species is one of the reasons it is virtually impossible to keep dragonflies in captivity since huge flight cages would be needed to allow room for them to behave and forage normally. When collecting small prey, dragonflies will chew quickly through the victim, drop the inedible wings, and fly to the next target. They usually carry large prey to a perch. Some of the clubtail dragonflies have very

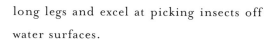

long legs and excel at picking insects off water surfaces.

The wings of the adult dragonfly are one of its most striking physical characteristics. Just as large and just as prominently displayed as those of butterflies and moths, dragonfly wings are at the same time less colorful but more intricate. As we have seen, the wing veins serve important functions both during the final molt and in flight. Since many dragonfly species can be identified from the wings alone, the arrangement of the major veins and cells can also determine family groupings. This means of classification, along with eye placement, became the basis for our pictorial key to the seven North American and

{ F I G U R E 40 }

A collage of the abdomens of several different skimmer species (family Libellulidae) showing differences in terminal appendages. The tails (abdomens) were digitally removed from the scanned images of live dragonflies. Scans provided by authors.

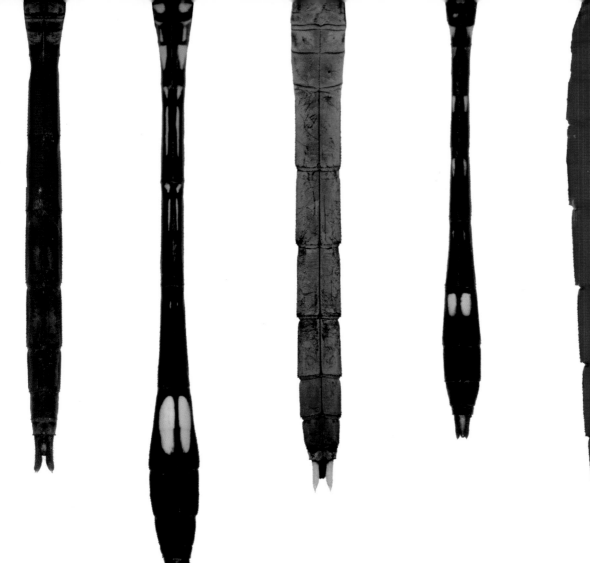

skimmer species tails (continued)

six European families of dragonflies. We marked the cells and veins of a front and rear pair of wings from a Roseate Skimmer (*Orthemis ferruginea*) using the nomenclature of Needham and Westfall in their 1955 book *A Manual of the Dragonflies of North America* *[Figure 36]*. This became our guide to identifying the adults from the dragonfly families of North America and Europe *[Figures 37, 38]*.

The abdomen of the adult still has ten segments but is now very elongated relative to the short, squat body of most larvae. The abdomen gives the dragonfly its characteristic shape and some of the vernacular names associated with it, such as horse stinger and devil's darning needle. The abdomen's major features are the secondary sex organs of the male, found on the underside of the second segment and the primary sex organs of both sexes on the ninth segment. Terminal appendages of the males, the claspers that project backward from the last segment of the abdomen, are species specific and often used in classification studies *[Figures 39, 40]*. They are arranged as two outer "cerci" and a median "epiproct," all of which function as a

means of capturing mates. Females may have structures on their heads and first sections of their thoraxes that accept the males' terminal appendages. These also act as a method of reproductive isolation, preventing males of the wrong species from successful mating. While not a perfect system, females of a different species are much harder for a male to capture.

The mating system of dragonflies is unique among insects and allows mating during flight. For mating to occur the male must move the tip of his abdomen forward and transfer a sperm packet from the organs located in the ninth segment of his abdomen to the secondary set of sex organs in the second segment. This frees the abdomen and the appendages on the tenth segment to capture a female.

Female dragonflies do not always have a choice of mate—the male will usually attempt to grab any female that passes by. Using the terminal appendages, the male locks the tip of his abdomen to the back of the female's head and may either fly in tandem with her or take her to a perch and alight. In either case, the female may immediately move her abdomen up to the

secondary organs of the male and accept the sperm pouch into her reproductive organs. In doing so, the dragonflies form a circle known as the wheel position [Figure 41]. The female may also manage to shake free without mating, but the male's grip is strong enough that Sidney Dunkle, a prominent dragonfly biologist, has noticed impressions on the heads of female clubtails made by the male claspers.

If the male is successful, he may continue to clasp the female and fly in tandem with her. This prevents other males from capturing her and superseding him in fertilization of the eggs. The male Common Green Darner and many species of skimmers will continue to clasp the female, even while she lays eggs [see Figure 20]. The males of other species release the female almost immediately but will usually guard her against the intrusion of marauding males while she lays eggs [see Figure 19]. Dragonfly mating behavior is an exciting field of study that has attracted talented students. Even so, numerous species still have no accounts of mating behavior on record.

Although an ancient group possessed of many unique adaptations, dragonflies still have much in common with the rest of the insect world. In spite of some misgivings and misunderstanding about them, they are not only harmless but also colorful and beautiful to look at. An increased appreciation of these delicate creatures not only improves and enriches our lives but also increases our awareness that they are as vulnerable as any animal to the depredations of the modern world.

{FIGURE 41}

Male and female Halloween Pennants (Celithemis eponina) *in the wheel position. This species ranges throughout the eastern United States. Photo © James L. Lasswell.*

CHAPTER FIVE

THE NATURAL HISTORY
OF DRAGONFLIES

Someone's first question on seeing a dragonfly might be, what species is it? Followed by, what is it doing? Dragonfly life history and behavior are rich, interesting subjects, and many scientific studies have been devoted to them. One monumental work, *Dragonflies: Behavior and Ecology of Odonata* by Philip Corbet, has summed up most of the important work on these insects, and anyone curious about the details of these topics can find an answer to virtually any question in the pages of his book. Here, an overview of the natural history of dragonflies provides some insight into how dragonflies live and features one area of behavior that still remains relatively unknown, the seasonal migration of dragonflies.

From the laying of eggs through the development of larvae, dragonflies need a source of fresh water. Since fresh water is a relative term for some species, it can take

{FIGURE 43}

Female Seaside Dragonlet (Erythrodiplax berenice), *found along the coastal United States from Texas to Maine and in some saline waters of the southwest.*
Photo © James L. Lasswell.

many forms. In general, each dragonfly species prefers a certain type of water body, and we can group species or even families according to these preferences. Brown cruisers and river cruisers (genera *Didymops* and *Macromia*) are found just where you would expect, in or near streams and rivers. Male *Macromia* will fly long stretches of a river in search of mates, but some will also patrol roads, perhaps attracted to the long open reaches unimpeded by vegetation. Brown cruisers are found in smaller streams and

{FIGURE 42}

Male Dragonhunter (Hagenius brevistylus), *found throughout the eastern United States. Scan provided by authors.*

{FIGURE 44}

Male Variegated Meadowhawk (Sympetrum corruptum). *Scan provided by authors.*

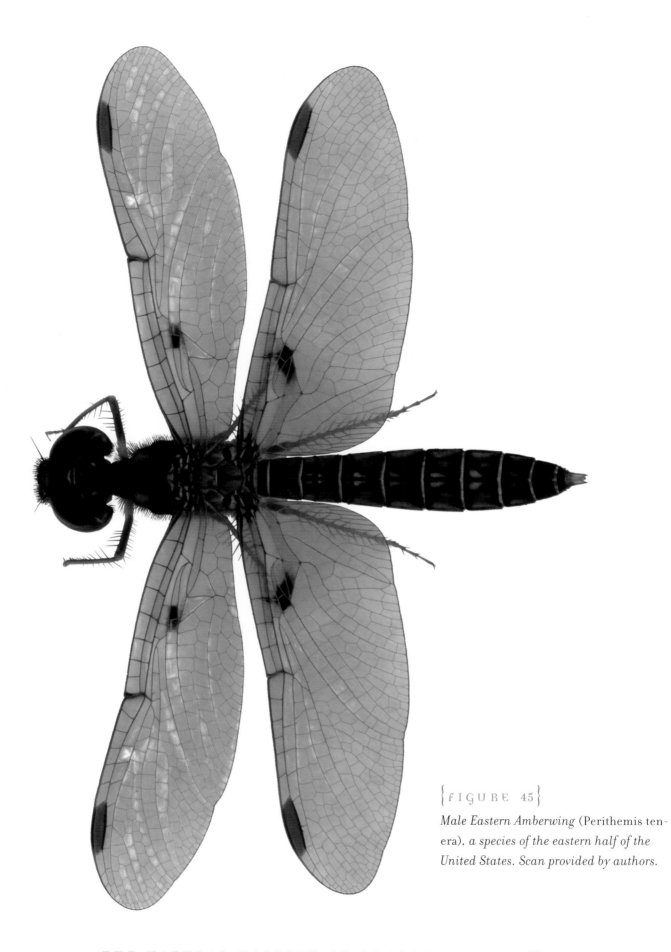

{ FIGURE 45 }

Male Eastern Amberwing (Perithemis tenera), a species of the eastern half of the
United States. Scan provided by authors.

{FIGURE 46}

The Frosted Whiteface (Leucorrhinia frigida), *a northeastern dragonfly species. Photo © Dave Westover.*

sometimes in the ponds made by streams. Some of the clubtails (family Gomphidae) may prefer unpolluted rivers; the Dragonhunter (*Hagenius brevistylus*) is one in particular [*Figure 42*]. Others lay their eggs in small ponds with muddy bottoms. Larvae of the Jade Clubtail (*Arigomphus submedianus*) are often one of the first colonizers of a new pond.

One species of dragonfly, the Seaside Dragonlet (*Erythrodiplax berenice*), breeds in brackish water and seawater [*Figure 43*]. While mainly a coastal species, it also lives inland in saline lakes and ponds in the southwestern United States. Very few insects have adapted to seawater, and since the family Libellulidae, to which this species belongs, is of comparatively recent origin, the ability to lay eggs in briny water is thought to be a new trait rather than a continuation from the primitive state.

Not every species is particular about water quality. We have recovered larvae of the Variegated Meadowhawk (*Sympetrum corruptum*) from water in the bottom of a muddy tire track [Figure 44]. The larvae of the tiny Eastern Amberwing (*Perithemis tenera*) can live in water that many species of dragonflies find unacceptable [Figure 45]. Waste-filled, algae-laden farm ponds saturated with the nitrates and phosphates from confined animal-feeding operations are often full of little amberwings. One year, a pond that usually contained a population of Widow Skimmer larvae (*Libellula luctuosa*) did not have any at all because a December rainstorm had added a superabundance of pollutants to the water. The amberwings, however, colonized the pond the next year and benefited from the lack of the larger predator dragonflies that did not survive.

Because adult dragonflies are such strong, capable fliers, they can disperse over long distances in a relatively short period of time. Weather and climate often determine the movement and distribution of various species. Some groups of dragonflies, notably the whitefaces (genus *Leucorrhinia*) [Figure 46] and many of the mosaic darners (genus *Aeshna*), are distinctly northern in distribution, while dragonflies like the Tropical King Skimmers (genus *Orthemis*) radiate from warmer localities. Dragonflies that stray from one locality to another during periods of favorable weather may lay eggs and set up temporary residence, but the climate in which the larvae develop will determine if they become successful, long-term residents. Shifts in range may become more apparent if global warming changes the climate enough for plants and animals to exploit new environments. Other human-induced changes, such as better habitat management and increased attention to natural areas, may also have an influence.

The need for water drives other aspects of dragonfly behavior. The male dragonfly commonly patrols streams, rivers, ponds, and lake shores in hopes of finding females. By choosing and, to varying degrees, defending territories, males may increase their odds of mating. Because of the aggressiveness of males, females are not usually found near water when not actively engaged in reproduction or laying eggs. They may be nearby in the vegetation or moving from

one location to another in search of a suitable laying site.

The aptly named Common Whitetail (*Libellula lydia*) is a familiar inhabitant of areas surrounding small ponds throughout most of the United States *[Figures 47, 48]*. Mature males of this species have a characteristic white coloration over most of their bodies and are easily seen as they dart low over the surface and edges of the water. Females make only short appearances over the water, where they are pursued and fought over by the resident males. It is not unusual, however, to walk through a wooded area near a pond or stream and find numbers of females and newly emerged males

A male Common Whitetail (Libellula lydia), *found throughout most of the United States. Scan provided by authors.*

foraging in open spots or perching on branches and foliage. They frequently visit residential backyard gardens as they move from pond to pond and might remain for a day or two. Mature males may also move cross-country in search of better water bodies and do not tend to linger in one spot if water is not present.

{FIGURE 48}
A female Common Whitetail (Libellula lydia). *Scan provided by authors.*

Adult dragonflies are very much the general predator and do not hesitate to attack anything they can catch, either large or small. Their excellent vision detects even the smallest prey, and their spiny legs make a natural net with which to capture the victim. Much has been made of their reputed ability to consume mosquitoes to the evident advantage of humans. Eden Emanuel Sarot in his 1958 treatise, *Folklore of the Dragonfly: A Linguistic Approach,* reported that upon seeing dragonfly swarms Indians in Mexico would celebrate and shout "se acaba la fiebre" or the "the end of the fever," referring, he believed, to the yellow fever spread by adult mosquitoes. He recounted that the Indians in Mexico had known for centuries that mosquitoes carried yellow fever and that dragonflies preyed on mosquitoes and could wipe out the fever if they showed up in large enough numbers. If true, this is rather remarkable considering the formal discovery of the relationship between yellow fever and mosquitoes by Walter Reed was not made until the twentieth century.

The degree to which adult dragonflies affect adult mosquito populations is hard to determine. They will certainly eat them if the opportunity arises, but most mosquitoes (the Asian tiger mosquito, *Aedes albopictus,* being a notable exception) forage at twilight or at night. Low-flying creatures, they prefer to remain near vegetation or structures of various sorts, places where they are most likely to find their victims and where it is difficult for dragonflies to navigate. In contrast, dragonflies are almost exclusively daytime fliers. While most species might feed into the dusk, even to the point of remaining in pools of light cast by car headlights, once true night falls they roost in trees and vegetation until morning. Unlike many other species of insects, dragonflies rarely fly at night.

Dragonfly larvae will also eat mosquito larvae whenever they can. In a rather detailed exercise of biological bookkeeping, Elsie Lincoln, a student of Philip Calvert, reared two large dragonflies—Black-tipped

{ FIGURE 49 }

A robber fly with a captured male Common Whitetail (Libellula lydia). *Photo © James L. Lasswell.*

An Eastern Pondhawk (Erythemis simplicicollis) *eating another dragonfly (identity unknown). Photo © Dave Westover.*

Darners, *Aeshna tuberculifera* [see Figures 119, 120]—from eggs to adults beginning in September 1935, and kept track of the number of mosquito larvae that each consumed. The first took 499 days and 15 molts to become an adult. In its last seven stadia it consumed 1,095 mosquito larvae and 180 mosquito pupae, not to mention 87 mayfly larvae, 20 damselfly larvae, 8 miscellaneous dragonfly larvae, 1 dytiscid beetle and 2 hydrophilid beetles, 2 backswimmers, 4 dixid stonefly larvae and 1 perlid stonefly larvae, 2 midge pupae, and 2 frog tadpoles except for the tails. The second larva developed into an adult in 492 days after 13 molts and consumed 1,334 mosquito larvae and 156.5 pupae along with a similar miscellany of other creatures.

A male Oklahoma Clubtail (Gomphus oklahomensis), a species whose range is restricted to Oklahoma, Arkansas, Louisiana, and Texas. Photo © Greg W. Lasley.

One of the most commonly asked questions regarding dragonflies is "how long do they live?" Unfortunately, this is one of the most difficult questions to answer. Since the larvae are relatively immobile and can be kept in captivity, we can give more exact answers regarding this life stage. The adults do not tolerate captivity, and all we can do is deduce their longevity from field experiments and observations.

Many things affect the life span of adults, not the least of which are weather and food supply. Dragonflies also fall prey to a number of other predators: the adults are commonly eaten by birds, spiders, robber flies, and other dragonflies *[Figures 49, 50]*, and the larvae are a favorite food of fish and in some areas of the world, people. They can, however, carry trematode worms, which may also parasitize the humans who eat them. In addition to trematodes, dragonflies may also carry protozoans called gregarines, but these are more common in damselflies, at least in our experience. Although they seldom kill their hosts, parasites still drain the insect's metabolism and certainly weaken it, making it more susceptible to other predators.

Given this list of possible mortality factors, and their impact as measured in the available scientific literature, Philip Corbet estimates that it takes a median of 14.2 days for a male dragonfly to reach sexual maturity once it has emerged to the adult stage. The dragonflies that survive this period can expect to live for 11 days longer, or a total of about 25 days. Maximum life spans are believed to be a little less than 40 days.

In most species of dragonflies, the larval stage lasts longer than the adult stage. There are reports of some species living in cooler climates that may take up to five years to become adults. While this is not as long as the periodical cicadas' larval phases—some as much as 13 to 17 years—it is certainly longer than most larval stages for other insects. At the other end of the spectrum, the rainpool gliders, which specialize in colonizing temporary water bodies, can become adults in under a month. In between these extremes, the duration of the larval stage will vary according to species or even within species. In 1937 and 1938, Philip Calvert reared nine larvae of the Southern Hawker (*Aeshna cyanea*) from eggs to adults. Even though the eggs were from the same clutch, and the larvae reared under almost identical conditions, the earliest larva to emerge took 187 days, while the last larva emerged in 385 days, a difference of 198 days or more than twice as long as the first larva.

Anyone who spends time near a swimming pool can attest to the frequent sightings of dragonflies that appear and survey the water. Some species do not defend territories on water or the margins of water but instead choose to forage both for food and mates over open ground. The Oklahoma Clubtail (*Gomphus oklahomensis*) is not an active flyer, preferring to move in short bursts and then perch on the ground or on

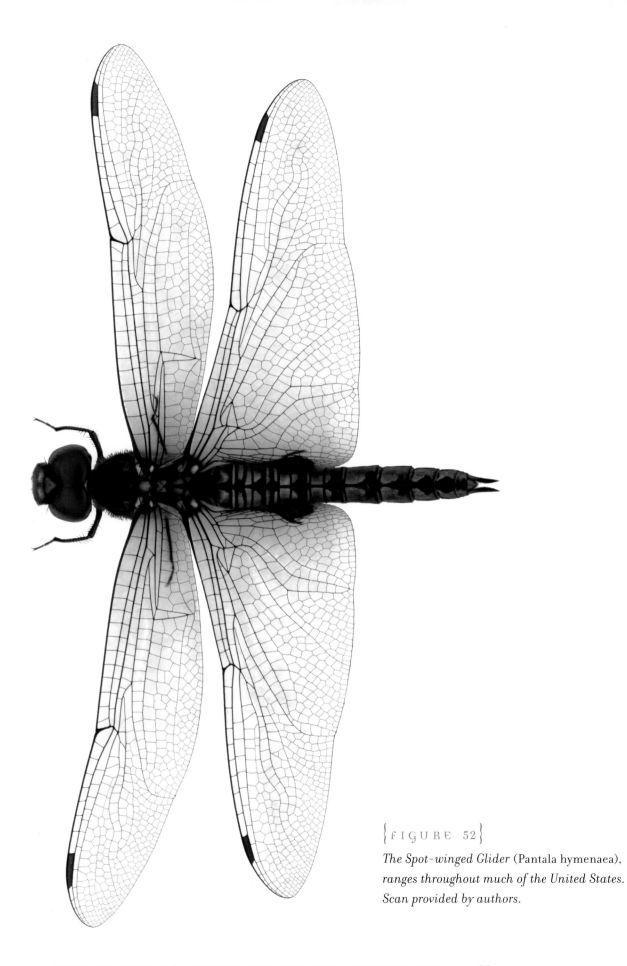

{FIGURE 52}

The Spot-winged Glider (Pantala hymenaea),
ranges throughout much of the United States.
Scan provided by authors.

low vegetation *[Figure 51]*. Narrow animal paths or bicycle trails a short distance from water can be full of adults chasing one another and small prey on the wing.

Many people have noticed the occasional large dragonfly swarm and wondered about it. Several scientists have researched the subject of dragonfly migration, and as with most research projects, they have created as many questions as they have answered. Massive swarms of dragonflies certainly appear, especially during the second half of the year. Traveling in a car to attend an exam being given to a Ph.D. student in 2002, one of us observed a swarm of Spot-winged Gliders (*Pantala hymenaea*) *[Figure 52]*, Wandering Gliders (*Pantala flavescens*), and Red Saddlebags (*Tramea onusta*) that was at least forty miles long. It began at sunrise over rural countryside and continued to the outskirts of a large urban area. Specimens were identified from the unfortunate victims collected from beneath the windshield wiper blades and hastily pocketed. During opening remarks at the exam, the student described himself as an insect pathologist. In the course of the exam he was handed the dragonfly remains

and asked, as an insect pathologist, his opinion of what killed them. Thinking it was a trick question he pored over the mangled specimens looking for the hidden clue. At length, his assessment of blunt trauma was correct, as was his conviction that it was a trick question.

There are many well-known examples of migration in animals: the swallows of San Juan Capistrano, California, and the elk herd of Jackson Hole, Wyoming. In the entomological world the best example we have is the Monarch butterfly, which makes an annual trek from the United States and Canada into the mountains of central Mexico in the autumn and returns each spring, re-colonizing the countryside on its northward flight.

Michael May, a professor of entomology at Rutgers University, studies the migratory behavior of dragonflies. Our discussion of this elusive subject is drawn from his research and writing.

Studying dragonfly migration is not as straightforward as it is with other animals, such as birds and mammals, where the conventional approach is to mark or tag an animal, release it, and hope it is recaptured at a later date (bird banding is an example). Recovering the tags or other markers at a distant location is absolute proof of movement. If a sufficient number of individuals are tagged, enough tags may be recovered over the course of time to provide a good assessment of how and when the population moves.

Longer lived migratory species, such as birds, may make the round trip between their seasonal areas repeatedly during their lifetimes, moving to and from their destinations with a regularity that we can sometimes track. Insects do not live long enough for one individual to make a complete trip, and thus they must make their migration journeys in stages that involve several generations.

The most well-known intergenerational insect migration is that of Monarch butterflies. These butterflies inhabit much of North America and produce multiple generations every year, but in the fall the last generation begins to move south. Studies have shown that their fall migratory flight has a large degree of predictability and that peak movement can usually be anticipated on a given date at a given geographic latitude. Here in Texas where we live, the Monarchs usually pass by in their largest numbers on October 6, filling the skies in the late afternoon. Most of the Monarchs on the eastern side of the Rocky Mountains end up congregating in the highlands of southern Mexico, where they spend the winter gathered together in just a few small areas. In the spring, these insects begin their return flight north, but few will make it all the way to the northern extent of their range. Instead, they begin laying eggs as they move north. Subsequent generations then complete the trip to their northern range, where they live and breed until the fall and the cycle begins again.

How do we know this? Monarchs are large and colorful. Their orange and black markings make them easily identifiable. They are reasonably easy to catch because they pause to feed on flowers and roost in large clusters in the evening. Many school children participate in Monarch marking events in the fall. They catch the butterflies and stick small paper tags to the wings. They record the relevant information and then release them to complete their journey.

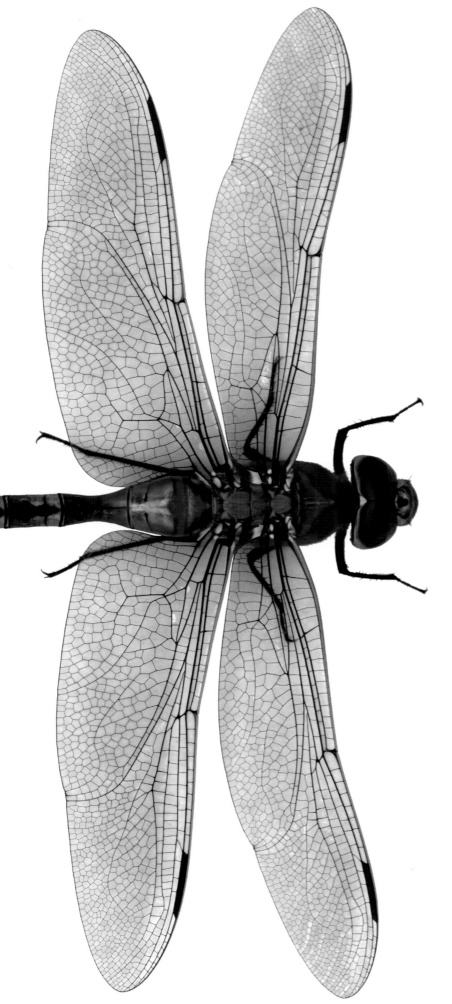

{ F I G U R E 53 }

A male Common Green Darner (Anax junius), *a species found throughout the United States and into southern Canada. Scan provided by authors.*

{ F I G U R E 54, *opposite* }

A female Common Green Darner (Anax junius). *Scan provided by authors.*

Once at their destination in Mexico, the Monarchs amass in large numbers. Searching for tags in these areas of concentration greatly increases the chances for their recovery.

So why not design a similar plan for dragonflies? We are reasonably certain some species do migrate (see Appendix D). Several regional organizations are already keeping detailed records of large-scale dragonfly movements, and their observations reveal that dragonflies have migratory patterns. Research publications also discuss observations and information that support the idea of mass migrations. Details on these movements, however, are still missing. Questions about why they migrate, where they go, how long they take, and other important aspects remain to be answered. We lack much of this information because of the difficulty in setting up a formal mark-release-recapture experiment, the major reason being that dragonflies are so hard to catch. It would take a significant number of marked dragonflies and a significant number of people looking for them in order for the experiment to work.

The development of an inexpensive, reliable means of marking sufficient numbers of dragonflies with an easily detected tag, without having to capture each individual, would be a very valuable contribution. If such a tool were available, the large numbers of people needed to spot the tags or marks could come from the pool of bird, butterfly, and dragonfly watchers already busy with their binoculars and nets.

In the absence of such a tool, how do we study dragonfly migration? The oldest approach, simply watching and counting them as they pass by, has yielded many interesting clues. Detailed observations of migratory events, accumulated over time, provide information that can be analyzed and used to guide other, more direct studies.

When we look for migrating dragonflies, location and season matter. In one interesting article, Robert Russell and his colleagues discussed how migrants appear to be especially affected by cold fronts, which have the effect of sweeping up and creating swarms. They also pointed out that geographical features, especially shorelines, influence the swarms, which may change directions to follow these features. Like birds, the behavior of dragonflies in migration is very susceptible to local conditions and at times movement may seem random.

Detailed observations of larvae or nymphs in ponds have been useful in determining the migration strategies of Common Green Darners [Figures 53, 54]. Robert Trottier demonstrated that two groups of darner larvae live in ponds in southern Canada. One group develops slowly, taking nearly a year to emerge as adults in the latter part of June or the first part of July. These adults remain in the vicinity and lay their eggs in late July and early August. The second group of larvae only requires three months to develop, from June to September. On emergence, the adults take wing and migrate from the area. Their offspring develop in a more southerly location, then begin to return the following year and start the cycle again in a strategy similar to that of Monarch butterflies.

Radar has also been used to track migrating insects. Without ground observers it is difficult to know which species of insect is in flight, but advanced radar technology can now detect wing-beat frequencies, which have subsequently been used to identify insect types. Researchers have previously tried to track pest species with radar, especially migratory locusts and moths, but dragonflies have occasionally been tracked as well. The advantage of this technology is that density, direction, and height of the dragonflies can be directly recorded. The disadvantage is that it is very expensive to implement.

In Appendix D is a form for making your own observations of dragonflies along with a list of suspected migratory species [Figures 55, 56]. If you spot a large assembly of dragonflies, fill in as much detail as you can; all the information is important, especially when compiled and compared with other reports. But do not be limited by the questions on the form. Other things that catch your attention or any additional thoughts may well matter, and it could be the first time someone has taken time to document a certain observation. Send your forms to the organization monitoring dragonflies in your area. If there is none, e-mail your forms to migration@dragonflies.org and we will forward them to interested researchers or groups that can make use of them.

WATCHING
DRAGONFLIES

Finding, identifying, and watching dragonflies are all part of a pastime that is gaining popularity. With the recent publication of some excellent field guides, even novices have a good chance of identifying the dragonflies they find. Fortunately, dragonflies are common and easy to see, especially on bright, warm, sunny days. They occur around practically any body of relatively clean water including roadside ditches, ponds, lakes, marshes, swamps, seeps, streams, and rivers. They can also be found quite some distance from water and are often seen in swarms over roadways, parking lots, and open fields. Even though dragonflies abound, most people tend not to notice them simply because they are not paying attention. Sometimes, however, dragonflies can be so plentiful that they are impossible to miss.

{FIGURE 57}

The smallest of the dragonflies in North America, the Elfin Skimmer (Nannothemis bella), *is found in the northeastern United States and in the states along the Atlantic and Gulf coasts to Louisiana. Photo © Robert A. Behrstock/Naturewide Images.*

When going out to watch dragonflies, take a few items to make the outing more enjoyable. We always carry water, a snack, insect repellent, and a copy of *Dragonflies through Binoculars: A Field Guide to Dragonflies of North America* by Sidney W. Dunkle. If you live in an area that has a regional field guide, be sure to bring it along (see the Bookshelf section at the end of this book). Rubber boots or hip waders are also a good idea, since the best places to search for dragonflies are around water, and it is always nice to go home with dry feet after a day out in the field. Last, a good pair of close-focus binoculars will prove invaluable. A number of models that range in price from reasonable to catastrophically expensive are available. Expensive binoculars are great, but even a modestly priced pair will allow a close enough view of a perched dragonfly to see its identifying features.

Dragonfly families have significant overlap in their habits and habitat preferences, but the differences between them are significant enough to warrant a separate discussion of each family. Armed with this information, dragonfly watchers will have a better idea of where to look and what to look for when out in the field.

{FIGURE 58}

A mature male Widow Skimmer (Libellula luctuosa) perched on a twig. Newly emerged males lack the white coloring (pruinescence) on the wings and abdomen. Photo © James L. Lasswell.

Currently, there are ten or eleven families of living dragonflies, although various authorities condense or expand them as new research and interpretations become available. These are: darners (Aeshnidae), tiger bodies (Chlorogomphidae), spiketails (Cordulegastridae), emeralds (Corduliidae), clubtails (Gomphidae), skimmers (Libellulidae), cruisers (Macromiidae), redspots (Neopetaliidae, which likely includes the eleventh family, Austropetaliidae), petaltails (Petaluridae), and southern emeralds (Synthemistidae). Of these, Libellulidae, Gomphidae, Aeshnidae, Corduliidae, Macromiidae, Cordulegastridae, and Petaluridae occur in the United States.

Skimmers (Family Libellulidae)

Surely the easiest to find and most numerous of the dragonflies are members of the family Libellulidae, generally called skimmers.

There are close to 1,000 species of skimmers worldwide with 106 species currently known from North America. Tropical species often show up in the southernmost parts of the United States, which enhances the number. Thirty-two species have very limited ranges in the United States, restricted primarily to Texas and/or Florida.

The skimmers are small to medium-sized dragonflies generally ranging from 2.5 to 5.0 centimeters (1 to 2 inches) in length. The smallest dragonfly found in North America is the Elfin Skimmer (*Nannothemis bella*) *[Figure 57]*. It measures only 20 millimeters (0.8 inches) in length and inhabits the eastern half of the United States from Alabama north into Maine and Canada and west to Wisconsin. The largest of the skimmers is the Great Pondhawk (*Erythemis vesiculosa*), which measures about 6.1 centimeters (2.4 inches) in length [see Figure 14]. The Great Pondhawk has been reported from a number of states in the southern United States but is apparently most commonly seen in Oklahoma, Texas, and the southern part of Florida.

Although they lack the metallic sheen of some other families, the skimmers as a group are among the most brightly colored of the dragonflies with hues ranging from muted browns or black to the full spectrum of the rainbow. Their wings are also frequently patterned in colors as well. Some species, as they mature, develop a pale, powdery appearance—called pruinescence—on the body, wings, or both. Pruinescence appears more typically in males and is usually more pronounced in older insects *[Figure 58]*. Some species change color as they mature *[Figures 59, 60]*.

As with many other creatures of nature male dragonflies are usually more brightly colored than females. In some species both the males and females sport the conspicuous wing patterning, with colors that range from black or dark brown in species such as the Desert Whitetail (*Libellula subornata*) *[Figures 61, 62]* and Filigree Skimmer (*Pseudoleon superbus*) *[Figures 63, 64]* to bright orange in the Flame Skimmer (*Libellula saturata*) *[Figures 65, 66]* or red in some of the saddlebags (genus *Tramea*) *[Figure 67]* and pennants (genus *Celithemis*) *[Figure 68]*.

Although some skimmers, like the gliders, may stay airborne for hours at a time, the majority will perch in obvious sight (the group is called perchers in Europe). Typically territorial in nature, male skimmers tend to stake out a portion of shoreline and fly back and forth, guarding it against other dragonflies. Flying regular beats, they often have a favorite twig, branch, log, or rock

A recently emerged male Red-tailed Pennant (Brachymesia furcata) displaying bright red coloration. Photo © James L. Lasswell.

A mature male Red-tailed Pennant (Brachymesia furcata). The thorax is no longer red but has darkened to an olive brown. Photo © Robert A. Behrstock/ Naturewide Images.

{FIGURE 61}

Note the dark band across each wing of this mature male Desert Whitetail (Libellula subornata). *Scan provided by authors.*

{FIGURE 62}

The female Desert Whitetail (Libellula subornata) *has two dark bands across each wing. Scan provided by authors.*

where they perch and look for intruders into their territory or for females with which to mate. They are relatively easy to approach when resting on their favorite perches, and even if startled they frequently return to the same or nearby spot.

The less colorful female skimmers often perch in much the same way as males but a short distance away from the water. Since they are not as territorial as the males, they

are not as prone to return to the same landing site when disturbed. The perching habit of these dragonflies makes them a favorite of dragonfly enthusiasts because they are quite easy to observe with a good pair of binoculars.

Members of this group are likely to be in backyards or parks, places that account for many of the interactions people have with dragonflies. Skimmers are not only easy to

A large part of both the front and hind wings of this male Filigree Skimmer (Pseudoleon superbus) *is dark colored. In the United States this species occurs only in Texas, New Mexico, and Arizona, but its range extends south into Mexico. Photo © Greg W. Lasley.*

find but also extremely entertaining to watch. Stake yourself next to a pond and observe them for a while. Every aspect of their behavior is engaging, whether feeding, mating, or guarding their territories.

The aerial antics of two rival males are something to see as they streak through the air in what seems to be an impossible flight display. They will often zip back and forth across the pond, with one in pursuit of the

The female Filigree Skimmer (Pseudoleon superbus) has a pretty, more intricate patterning on her wings than the male. Scan provided by authors.

other, then in a sudden blur disappear straight into the air. The winner of the dogfight usually returns to the pond within a short time. Toward the end of the summer many dragonflies carry battle scars from these and other aerial encounters, and their wings are often tattered. On one occasion, we observed a couple of male Twelve-spotted Skimmers (*Libellula pulchella*) *[Figure 69]* that were still able to fly, each with almost 90 percent of a hind wing missing.

Clubtails (Family Gomphidae)

This family constitutes a large group of dragonflies whose main feature is the enlargement of three of its abdominal segments (seven through nine). This characteristic, which is more prominent in males, gives the abdomen a club-like appearance—thus the name clubtail. The number of

{ F I G U R E 66 }

The wings of the female Flame Skimmer (Libellula saturata) *have some orange in them, but it is not as extensive as that of the male. Scan provided by authors.*

{ F I G U R E 67 }

The beautiful male Striped Saddlebags (Tramea calverti) *has red marking along the base of its hind wings. This species is found primarily from south Texas into Mexico. Scan provided by authors.*

{ F I G U R E 65 }

The basal half of the wings, the portion closest to the body, of the male Flame Skimmer (Libellula saturata) *is a beautiful burnt orange color. Photo © Greg W. Lasley.*

Amanda's Pennant (Celithemis amanda) *is another species with colorful red marking on the basal section of the hind wings. This species ranges from eastern Texas along the Gulf and Atlantic coast states into South Carolina. Photo © Robert A. Behrstock/Naturewide Images.*

species in this group currently approaches 1,000, with 12 genera and 98 species now recognized in North America. The clubtails are on average a little larger than the skimmers, ranging from 3.8 to 6.6 centimeters (1.5 to 2.6 inches) in length.

Clubtails, such as the Pronghorn Clubtail (*Gomphus graslinellus*), perch in the open on rocks or logs along shorelines or in the middle of streams, on sandy beaches, or on twigs and leaves *[Figure 70]*. They tend to be very wary and often fly when approached, seldom returning to the same spot. Yet clubtails can be quite numerous in some locales and, with a good pair of binoculars, fairly easy to observe from a distance.

{F I G U R E 69, *above*}

The Twelve-spotted Skimmer (Libellula pulchella) *lives throughout the United States and
also in southern Canada. Scan provided by
authors.*

{F I G U R E 70}

The Pronghorn Clubtail (Gomphus graslinellus) *is found from central Texas north
through the central part of the United States
and into Canada. Scan provided by authors.*

The dark brown and bright yellow Common Sanddragon (Progomphus obscurus).
Photo © Greg W. Lasley.

This interesting group of dragonflies has acquired some colorful English names for species such as the Dragonhunter, the largest of the clubtails [see Figure 42], and for several genera, including sanddragons (genus *Progomphus*) [Figure 71], spinylegs (genus *Dromogomphus*) [Figure 72], and snake-tails (genus *Ophiogomphus*) [Figure 73]. Clubtails are typically colored in earth tones, which helps camouflage them while they are perched. There are some exceptions, such as the Serpent Ringtail (*Erpetogomphus lampropeltis*), a species whose males may have a blue to bluish-green thorax [Figure 74].

Clubtails present several difficulties to those who study them. Besides being fairly well camouflaged, many species are rather reclusive. Some perch in vegetation or on the ground, especially near water, and remain undiscovered until disturbed. Others are crepuscular, meaning they fly only during the early morning or late evening. Finally, they are among the most difficult dragonflies to accurately and

{ F I G U R E 72, *above* }

The Black-shouldered Spinyleg
(Dromogomphus spinosus) *is one of three*
spinylegs found in North America. The long,
comb-like hind femur is unique to this genus
of dragonflies. Scan provided by authors.

{ F I G U R E 73 }

The beautifully colored Sinuous Snaketail
(Ophiogomphus occidentis) *is a resident of*
the northwestern United States and south-
western Canada. Scan provided by authors.

This clubtail with the bright blue and black thorax and bright blue eyes is the Serpent Ringtail (Erpetogomphus lampropeltis). *Its range in the United States is limited to the southwest, where it is considered uncommon. Photo © Robert A. Behrstock/Naturewide Images.*

completely identify, even with a specimen in hand.

Although many clubtails spend a great deal of time perched during the day, some are fairly active fliers. The males of species such as the Eastern Ringtail (*Erpetogomphus designatus*) [Figure 75] and the leaftails (genus *Phyllogomphoides*) [Figure 76] will at times patrol back and forth along a stretch of river or stream for a considerable length of time. Eventually, however, they will land on a favorite rock or twig and offer a good view.

Clubtail larvae have many of the cryptic habits of their parents and may burrow into mud to be completely buried or have only their abdomens pushed above the bottom sediments [Figure 77].

{ F I G U R E 75, *above* }

The Eastern Ringtail (Erpetogomphus designatus), *typically found along rocky riffle
areas of rivers and streams, is the only ringtail found east of Texas. Scan provided by
authors.*

{ F I G U R E 76 }

The Five-striped Leaftail
(Phyllogomphoides albrighti) *is a beautifully marked gomphid. The eighth abdominal segment of the males is widely flanged.
Scan provided by authors.*

{ FIGURE 77 }

A typical clubtail larva showing the tubular abdomen and large, straight antennae. Most clubtail larvae are burrowers. Scan provided by authors.

Darners (Family Aeshnidae)

This family contains many large species of dragonflies and a few small ones. On average, the largest dragonflies in North America are aeshnids. They range from 6.1 to 10.9 centimeters (2.4 to 4.3 inches) in length, with the majority being between 6.4 and 8.9 centimeters (2.5 to 3.5 inches). Known as darners in North America and hawkers in Europe, this group has over 400 described species. Some 10 percent of these, in 13 genera, occur in North America.

Many of the adults in this group are colored in combinations of blue, green, black, and brown, although there are some emphatic exceptions, such as the Comet Darner (*Anax longipes*) with its bright brick-red abdomen [*Figure 78*]. All are strong fliers and fierce predators. The largest member is the Giant Darner (*Anax walsinghami*), which is more than 10.9 centimeters (4.3 inches) in length [*Figure 79*]. In the United States, it lives in the desert southwest from extreme west Texas to California.

When at rest, darners hang vertically, usually from tree branches or on small tree

{FIGURE 78}

Found in the eastern one-third of the United States, the aptly named Comet Darner (Anax longipes) sports a long, red abdomen, looking much like the tail of a comet. It is the only darner with red markings. Scan provided by authors.

{FIGURE 79}

The Giant Darner (Anax walsinghami) is our largest darner, measuring a grand 10.9 centimeters (4.3 inches) in length. It is an uncommon species in the southwestern United States. Scan provided by authors.

trunks, bushes, or even weeds. In addition to their large size and strong flight, darners are easily distinguished from other families of dragonflies because their very large eyes fit tightly together on top of their head. The other families have either widely separated eyes or eyes that barely meet.

The most common of the darners is the aptly named Common Green Darner (*Anax junius*), which ranges throughout the United States and north into the southern provinces of Canada [see Figures 53, 54]. One of the more rarely seen species of dragonflies in the United States is the Amazon Darner (*Anax amazili*). This species has been reported only sporadically in the United States, from Florida, Louisiana, and Texas. One of the sightings was of a male that had been captured by a Purple Martin and was about to become dinner for the bird's offspring [*Figure 80*].

Darner larvae are long-bodied and may be active predators, especially in small ponds that do not have fish. The larval Common Green Darner stalks its prey in a manner reminiscent of a praying mantis [*Figure 81*]. Its head swivels to bring its large eyes to bear on any object of interest.

Emeralds (Family Corduliidae)

The emeralds are a small family related to the cruisers (Family Macromiidae). Some scientists believe that the cruisers do not belong in a family of their own but in a subfamily under Corduliidae (or Libellulidae). Many species of both families have striking green eyes. The emeralds are very similar in size to the clubtails, from about 3.3 to 6.6 centimeters (1.3 to 2.6 inches) long. Of approximately 275 named species worldwide, about 50 are found in North America.

Except for a few species, members of this group are generally rare and difficult to find. Some are very secretive, some have short flight seasons (the length of time they can be found each year), and some fly for only short periods of time each day. The baskettails (genus *Epitheca*) are the exception for they range throughout the eastern and southeastern United States and are quite common around both ponds and lakes, especially during the early part of the summer.

{FIGURE 80}

This remarkable photo of a Purple Martin feeding an Amazon Darner (Anax amazili) *to its young was one of only six sightings reported in the United States at the time. In 2003 and 2004, however, there were numerous sightings of the Amazon Darner in deep south Texas.*
Photo © Curtis E. Williams.

Taxonomists have assigned some interesting English names to various species in this family. Names such as boghaunters (genus *Williamsonia*) and shadowdragons (genus *Neurocordulia*) evoke the shadowy, mist-filled moors of England. The Orange Shadowdragon (*Neurocordulia xanthosoma*) from the south-central part of the United States is indeed a shadowy figure, flying each day for only a short time at sunrise and then again after sunset for about the last thirty to forty minutes of light *[Figures 82, 83]*. These are exceptionally beautiful dragonflies even though they are not brightly colored at all.

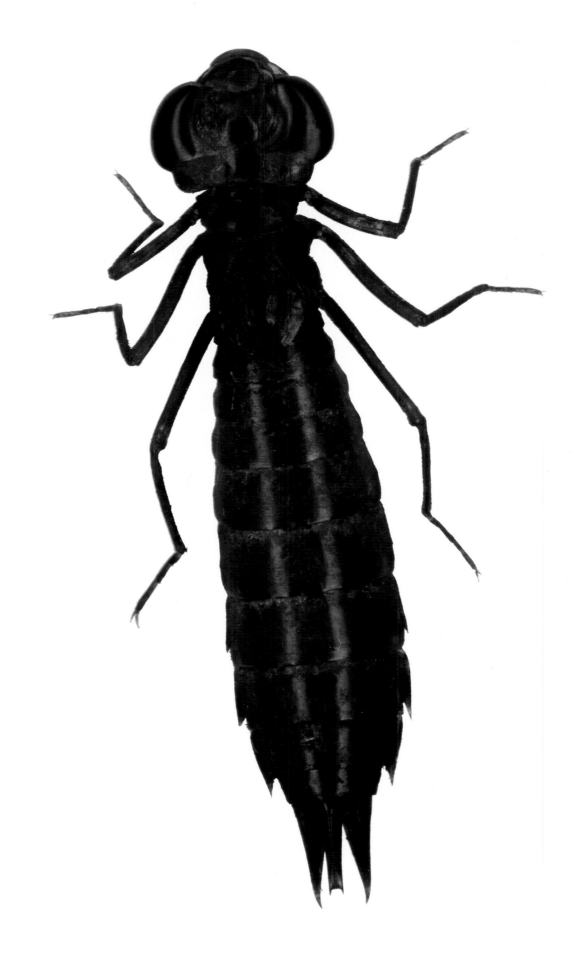

{ F I G U R E 81, *opposite*}

Top scan of a Common Green Darner larva (Anax junius) *showing the elongated shape typical of the family Aeshnidae. Scan provided by authors.*

{ F I G U R E 82, *above*}

Male Orange Shadowdragon (Neurocordulia xanthosoma). *Scan provided by authors.*

{ F I G U R E 83, *right*}

Female Orange Shadowdragon (Neurocordulia xanthosoma). *Scan provided by authors.*

{ F I G U R E 86 }

The Prince Baskettail (Epitheca princeps), a
common resident throughout most of the
eastern one-half of the United States. Scan
provided by authors.

The family name "emerald" recalls the gem of the same name, and the eyes of some of the emeralds almost match the brilliance of these lovely colored stones [Figure 84]. The emerald green eyes of species such as the Texas Emerald (*Somatochlora margarita*) [Figure 85] are so bright they can easily be seen even when the dragonflies are in flight. The Texas Emerald flies for only about two months during the middle part of the summer, and its range is restricted to a small area of the piney woods of east Texas and western Louisiana. These dragonflies, like many of the emeralds, have a pretty iridescent green or bronze sheen on their bodies.

Some of the emeralds also have patterned wings. The patterning is quite variable, from the subtle markings of the Orange Shadowdragon to the more extensive patterning found on the Prince Baskettail (*Epitheca princeps*), which itself varies widely within the species [Figure 86]. In the southeastern United States, Prince Baskettails have large dark spots on their wings and were at one time considered a separate species, *Epitheca regina*, but are now called a subspecies.

Cruisers (Family Macromiidae)

Another small family of dragonflies is the Macromiidae, whose English names include the brown cruisers (genus *Didymops*) and river cruisers (genus *Macromia*). The name "cruiser" reflects the habits of the adults, who are seldom at rest as they patrol the reaches of a river or stream. Some scientists reduce this family to subfamily status and place it under either the family Corduliidae or Libellulidae. Depending on an author's view of dragonfly classification, between 80 and 130 species can be assigned to this group. Only nine species in two genera occur in the United States.

The dragonflies in the genus *Didymops* are muted in color, but those in the genus *Macromia* are striking. Adults are usually yellow and black striped, like spiketails, but have a single yellowish thoracic stripe where spiketails have two stripes. Like emeralds, some cruisers have emerald green eyes so luminous they can be seen even at a distance as the insect flies by. Some also have the emeralds' iridescent sheen on the thorax. Relative to other dragonflies, a cruiser's middle and front legs are especially long, giving it a "spidery" appearance.

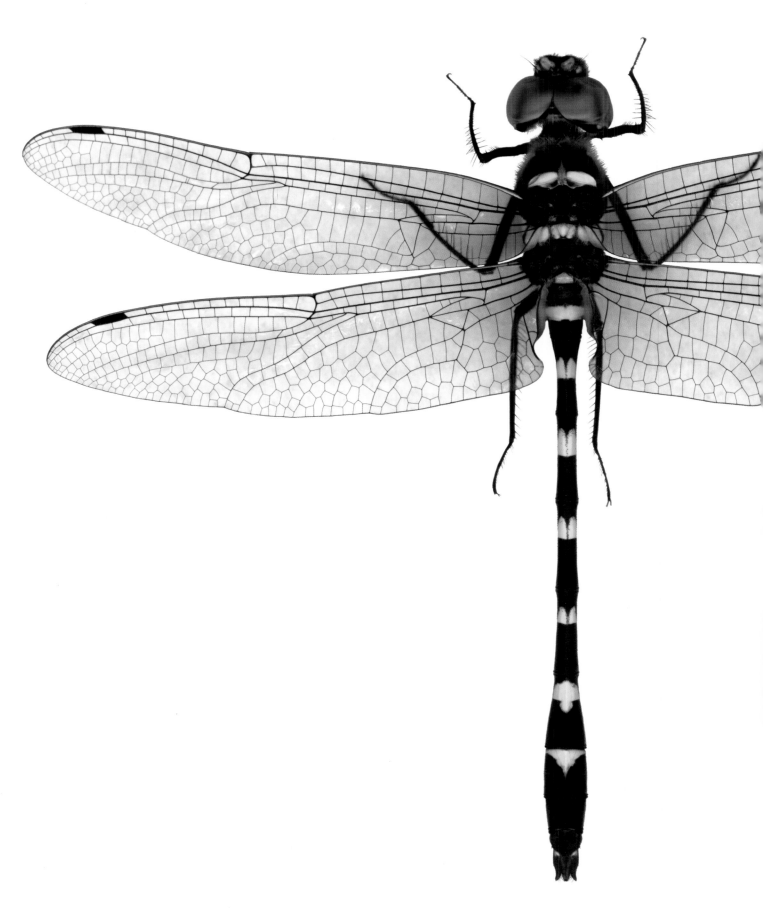

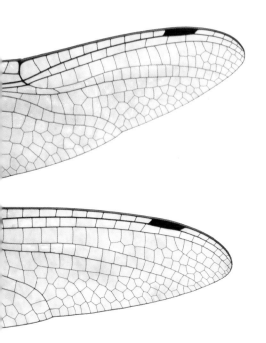

{FIGURE 87}

The Illinois River Cruiser (Macromia illinoiensis) *has brilliant green eyes that can be easily seen when these strikingly colored dragonflies are in flight. This is a common species found throughout the eastern half of the United States and north into Canada. Scan provided by authors.*

Species such as the Illinois River Cruiser (*Macromia illinoiensis*) often move in large numbers back and forth along tree-lined roads or open forests [*Figure 87*]. At rest, they hang vertically, like darners, and are especially viewable by humans.

Cruiser larvae are rounded and, like the adults, have long spidery legs, resembling something of a miniature snow crab. The larvae live at the bottoms of streams and rivers and are not often seen.

Spiketails (Family Cordulegastridae)

The spiketail family, also referred to as gold-enrings or biddies, is another small group with eight species in one genus, *Cordulegaster,*

in the United States. Scientists dispute the taxonomy of this group, and some of these species may soon be moved to other genera.

The spiketails actually get their name from the spike-like ovipositor that females use to lay their eggs in the soil along the edges of shallow forest streams. Moving back and forth over a likely spot, the female orients herself vertically and bobs up and down, driving the armored ovipositor down and releasing the eggs into the soil along the stream's edge.

When at rest, spiketails tend to perch on stems and twigs where they hang at an oblique angle to the ground. They are quite wary and when disturbed may simply fly up

{FIGURE 88}

*This large dragonfly (8.4 centimeters or 3.3 inches), the Arrowhead Spiketail (*Cordulegaster obliqua), *has brilliant blue eyes that contrast with the overall color of the body. The arrowhead-shaped yellow markings on the abdomen are responsible for its name. Scan provided by authors.*

over the treetops and disappear. Of the eight species found in North America, six are found in the east and two in the west. Although Say's Spiketail (*Cordulegaster sayi*) is a close rival, our favorite among the spiketails is surely the Arrowhead Spiketail (*Cordulegaster obliqua*) [Figure 88]. A series of yellowish, arrowhead-shaped marks on the surface of its abdomen give it its English name. The spiketails are not the most common of dragonflies, so some effort is needed to see them, but it is worth the work. The larvae of this group normally reside in streams, buried in the sediment with their head and eyes projecting out.

Petaltails (Family Petaluridae)

Members of the Petaluridae family, or petaltails (sometimes called graybacks),

are believed to be the oldest living species in the dragonfly suborder Anisoptera, much like the *Epiophlebia,* the surviving genus of the even older suborder Anisozygoptera. The petaltails, whose dinosaur-era fossils frequently turn up, may represent the last of an ancient group.

The English name is derived from the petal-shaped appendages on the abdominal tips of several representatives of this family. Petaltails are one of only two dragonfly families in the United States that have widely separated eyes, the other being the family Gomphidae. Eleven species in five genera still exist, while a number of extinct petulurid species have been found fossilized in Mesozoic strata.

Another of our favorite dragonflies belongs to this family. It is the Gray Petaltail (*Tachopteryx thoreyi*) [Figure 89]. Unlike skimmers the petaltails are not colorful at all; in fact, they have cryptic coloration that allows them to blend into their habitat [Figure 90]. There are only eleven species of petaltails in the world with two of these occurring in the United States, one eastern and one western.

Looking at a petaltail today, one gets an impression of how ancient dragonflies

must have lived and behaved in their primeval habitats. Hanging from a tree trunk in a swampy river bottom, completely motionless, with its subdued colors conforming to the earth tones of the wilderness, a Gray Petaltail gives the appearance of a prehistoric creature, far removed from its colorful, active contemporaries. Yet petaltails are not wary at all and are extremely easy to approach and observe. The problem, though, is finding them because they are somewhat local in distribution.

Gray Petaltails are quite common in parts of the Big Thicket in east Texas during

The Gray Petaltail's usual perching spot is on the trunks of trees where they blend in well with the background. Photo © Jack Brady.

the early part of the year, and we have actually had several of them fly up and land on us *[Figures 91, 92]*. The Gray Petaltail's favorite perch is to situate itself vertically on a tree trunk, where it is almost invisible. If discovered, it will usually permit a close enough approach for a good look and a good photograph (see Chapter 9). Do not be surprised if it flies off the tree and lands on you as you move toward it. If it does, you can sometimes gently shoo it off, and it will fly right back to the tree trunk. This is also a trait of the Black Petaltail (*Tanypteryx hageni*), which can be found in the Pacific

{FIGURE 91}

The Gray Petaltail is not bashful and will often land on people as they walk through the woods. One particular petaltail, perched on the trunk of a pine tree, was supposed to be the subject of a photograph showing it in its natural habitat. But before the photo could be taken, it flew down and landed on a pants pocket. Photo © Jack Brady.

Northwest, and one of the characteristics that make petaltails so endearing.

The larvae of these dragonflies are burrowers and referred to by some as semiaquatic. While studying the Gray Petaltail, Sidney Dunkle, the author of *Dragonflies Through Binoculars,* determined that the larvae could survive without being completely submerged in water if they were covered in wet detritus. Although they did not burrow, they did effectively hide.

{ FIGURE 92 }

Head-on photo of the "pocket petaltail" in Figure 92. Photo © James L. Lasswell.

Enjoy!

If you start watching dragonflies, you will, like us, surely begin to keep a "life list" of the dragonfly species you see. You will also likely find yourself searching for the more uncommon groups, such as the emeralds, spiketails, and petaltails. We have a co-worker who was first introduced to dragonflies in the spring of 2002 and soon began taking his two daughters on outings to watch them. His daughters enjoyed it so much that the family now takes frequent dragonfly watching trips to lakes, ponds, and rivers throughout central Texas. As he and his daughters have discovered, watching dragonflies can be a lot of fun. Try it!

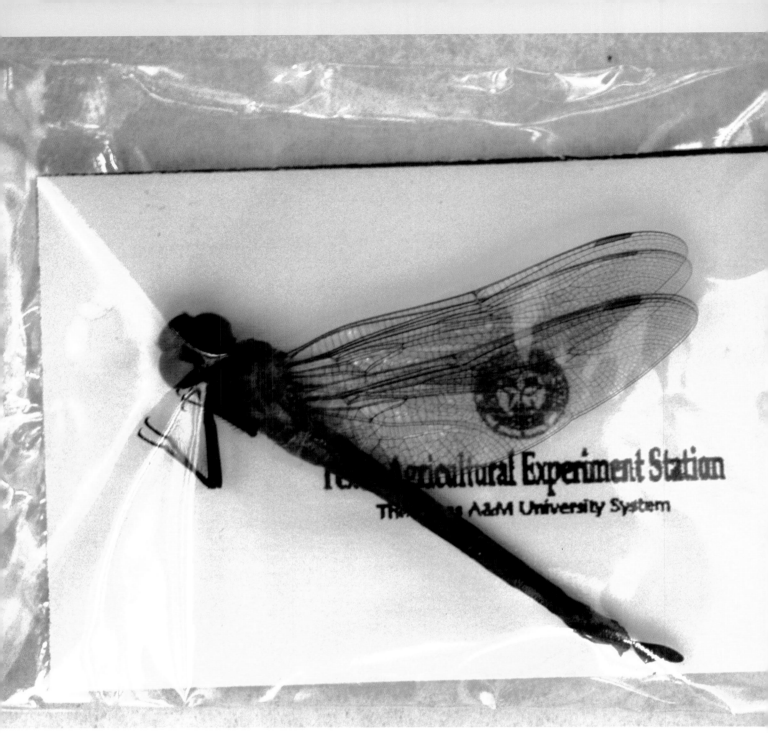

CHAPTER SEVEN

COLLECTING
DRAGONFLIES

The stereotypical entomologist, wearing a pith helmet and swinging a white net, is an old Hollywood mainstay and a familiar image in the public's mind since at least the Victorian era. In the nineteenth century, every gentleman scientist had a requisite butterfly collection hanging on his wall. In today's environmentally sensitive world, collecting specimens is often viewed as a politically incorrect activity.

In reality, insect collections have been at the foundation of entomological research for centuries. A correctly labeled and properly maintained collection is far from being a dusty assortment of moldering relics that have little value except to the collector. Scientists have gathered a tremendous amount of information from collected specimens. Comparing specimens helps determine species, and studying species in detail permits careful measurement, close analysis of colors or markings, and in the modern world, DNA sampling. Ultimately,

this information can increase our understanding and help locate and conserve dragonfly populations and habitat.

Collecting a series of specimens is more valuable than having a single example, and the labels on the specimens are just as important as the specimens themselves. Combined with the insects' physical data, information about date of collection, locality, and habitat allows scientists to determine averages of such things as body characteristics and activity dates as well as to assess geographical ranges. When questions arise or new technology materializes, the insects are physically present in the collection to help resolve any issues or participate in new studies. If properly cared for, the specimens may last indefinitely. There are specimens of insects still in existence that were caught and mounted on pins in the 1700s. (The oldest known specimen is a butterfly in the Oxford University Museum of Natural History with a collection date of 1702).

Before embarking on a collection of dragonflies, the collector should consider some points of practical nature and social

{DETAIL OF FIGURE 93}
See in full on page 146.

context. The practical issues revolve around the fact that both pinned and acetone-preserved adult dragonflies are extremely fragile and difficult to maintain in a collection. Another practical issue in preserving adult dragonflies is color loss. This can be extreme, especially the loss of eye color. Color loss can be reduced somewhat by acetone preservation, but the overall result is far from perfect. The immature stages of dragonflies, the larvae, also present some storage problems that we will discuss later in this chapter.

Acquiring and maintaining an insect collection, while a very enjoyable activity, has acquired an increasing burden of responsibility in modern society. Although it is not possible to please everyone, a little courtesy and forethought will go a long way in accommodating the sensibilities of those who would rather watch dragonflies and other insects fly freely than to collect them. Toward this end, the Dragonfly Society of the Americas (DSA) has drawn up a document outlining the responsibilities of the dragonfly collector to the dragonfly, the environment, and to fellow citizens. This document is presented in Appendix C and should be read and understood before taking on the responsibility of a collection.

Collecting Adults

The best way to collect adult dragonflies is the hard way—with a net. Of all the insects, dragonflies are probably the most elusive to the collector. It takes time and patience to be successful. But with the correct tools and some practice and care, the collector can improve the odds of success considerably. The main tool is an aerial net with a lightweight bag and a sturdy handle. It helps to have a green bag if you are collecting near vegetation, which is almost always the case. Dragonflies can still see the bag, but perhaps it is not as noticeable as a white bag. The sturdy handle allows for fast swings. If the handle is not up to the task, the bag will part company with the handle, usually out into the deepest part of the pond or fastest part of the river. Be careful that the net handle is not too long for the same reason. Long-handled nets for collecting in forest canopies require skillful use if they are not to break. A wide diameter rim is also desirable with 46 centimeters (18 inches) being a good size.

Once collected, the specimen needs to be bagged properly to prevent damage. Small, zippable, plastic freezer bags are ideal for this purpose. A bag 7-by-15 centimeters (3-by-6 inches) will hold even the largest dragonfly. In our collecting experience, we have developed a system that protects the dragonfly in the plastic freezer bag. We place the bag containing the dragonfly inside a hard plastic sandwich container, which then fits in a small fabric cooler that has a sealed, frozen ice brick in the bottom. We put a water bottle between the ice brick and the plastic sandwich container to buffer the dragonfly from direct cold. It is cold enough not to move and hurt itself in the plastic bag, but not so cold as to be affected if released.

Several useful tactics will aid in capturing dragonflies. With a few minutes of observation, you can sometimes determine the preferred flight path of the target dragonfly. If it flies a particular route, you can capture it simply by standing near this route and waiting for an opportunity to swing. Even so, only about 10 to 20 percent of swings will be successful on an average day. While this varies from person to person, be patient. Do not become discouraged by missing, and do not worry about how long it takes. We have actually spent almost two hours trying to capture a particular dragonfly. We collected our first Swamp Darner (a female) in 1996, but six years passed before we were able to add a male Swamp Darner to the Digital Dragonflies collection. As luck would have it, on that day they were easy to catch; we collected several and many more passed within easy net range.

It is much easier to catch dragonflies at rest than in flight. If you see one perched in an accessible area, approach it slowly and quietly, from the rear if possible. A smaller percentage of the compound eyes look rearward, so the dragonfly is less likely to become alarmed and take flight. Wearing drab or even camouflage clothing helps make the collector less conspicuous. Dragonflies see color quite well and may shy away from brightly colored clothing. When swinging at a perched dragonfly, plan which way to make the swing to optimize the chances for success, from above or sideways. Check for briars or anything else that might snag the net and let the intended quarry escape.

Specimen Number: eh_6aa,ta

Species: Epiaeschna heros   **Sex (m/f):** f

Date Collected: 04-10-02   **Collector:** Forrest Mitchell

Location (County, State): San Jacinto Co, TX

Nearest Body of Water: Big Creek

Nearest Road: State Hwy 150   **Time Collected:** 2:10 Pm

Weather: Partly Cloudy, Warm   80+ degrees

Habitat Notes: Narrow dirt road thru thick pine forest!

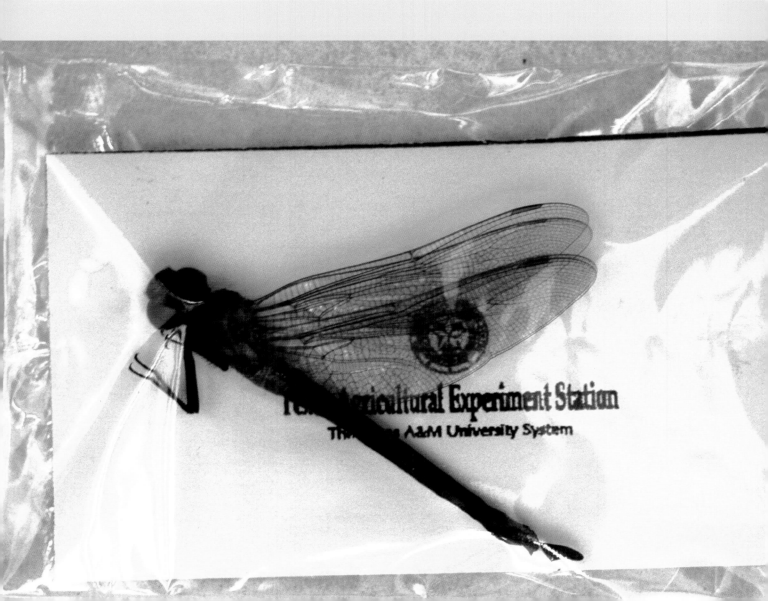

When successful, remove the dragonfly from the net taking care not to damage the legs or wings. The best way is to reach into the net and gently fold all four wings up over the body. In this manner, the wings can be held between the thumb and forefinger and used as a handle to remove the dragonfly from the net. The wings are sturdy enough to withstand this if done carefully, and if the specimen is released immediately it can be done with no harm to the dragonfly. The wings are quite strong, but if they are bent at too great an angle they will break. Dragonflies also have a lot of spines on their legs that can become entangled in the net. These must be carefully extracted so as not to damage them when the specimen is removed.

It is entirely possible to injure a dragonfly during collection, so be sure you want it before catching it. If you are keeping the dragonfly for later use, place it into the plastic bag with its wings still folded over its back. Then gently flatten the bag just far enough to keep the dragonfly immobile. Although dragonflies cannot fold their wings over their backs on their own, it does not appear to hurt them for the collector to do so. Do not place the specimen into the bag with its wings spread. This enables it to thrash about, and it can easily harm itself. Use only one bag per specimen. If two specimens are placed in the same bag, they will chew on each other when they come in contact. After placing the dragonfly in the bag, put it in a cool, dark area such as an ice chest where it will not be crushed. Exposure of the dragonfly to direct sunlight while in the bag can be lethal in a relative short period of time.

Once the specimen is back at home or the lab, it may be photographed or scanned (Chapter 9), preserved and placed into a collection, or if unneeded and well taken care of, released. Avoid releasing dragonflies in areas where they do not naturally reside for reasons outlined in the DSA statement on collections (Appendix C). In

{FIGURE 93}

Bottom half of photo: an acetone-dried female Swamp Darner (Epiaeschna heros) *in an Odonata envelope. Top half of photo: the card with collection data for the preserved specimen. Photo © James L. Lasswell.*

general, if the specimen is not to be released where it was captured, it is best to place it into a collection.

Another means of collecting adult dragonflies is to capture and rear the larvae (see Chapter 8). Many species can be successfully reared, especially if their development is fairly advanced when they are collected. The teneral (newly emerged) adults will not have all the color of a mature adult until the exoskeleton hardens, and even then it may take some days for colors to fully develop. Keeping adults alive in captivity is seldom practical, and they should be either released soon after emergence or added to a collection.

Preserving Adults

To kill collected specimens, collectors use standard insect killing jars charged with either cyanide or, preferably, ethyl acetate. The specimen may also be frozen and removed when the collector is ready to curate it. To curate an insect specimen means to prepare it properly for addition to and maintenance in a museum or insect collection. Some dragonflies die when exposed to freezing temperatures for only a short period of time; others do not and may have to be left in the freezer for several hours. The preferred method for best color retention is immersion in acetone. Acetone is available at most hardware stores, but it has toxic fumes and is flammable—use it carefully.

Air Drying and Acetone Drying

Scientists who research dragonflies do not normally pin them but instead place them in transparent plastic envelopes called Odonata envelopes, which are supported by heavy cards that contain all the pertinent collecting information [Figure 93]. Specimens for this purpose are normally air-dried or acetone-dried. When immersing a specimen in acetone, place it first in a paper or glassine envelope, the type used by stamp and coin collectors, and leave it for 24 to 48 hours, depending on the size of the dragonfly. The paper is undamaged by the acetone and keeps the dragonfly properly composed, meaning the legs and wings are not askew. Because dragonfly specimens are extremely brittle, using Odonata envelopes reduces the storage requirements from that of pinned specimens and also keeps in one place all the parts of the specimen that may, and likely will, fall off over time.

The card may be computer printed or hand-written. If it is placed into the envelope so that the specimen does not obscure the collection data, neither the card nor the specimen needs to be removed to see the information. The transparent envelope affords a clear view of the specimen, even under a dissecting microscope. If the dragonfly must be removed, do it very carefully and make sure to return any loose parts to the plastic bag. Each part of the dragonfly specimen has value.

Pinning

If the dragonfly is to be pinned in a box or tray, acetone treatment is not warranted. Acetone may corrode the pin, and it is difficult to immerse a spread dragonfly. When pinning a dragonfly, the pin should be placed through the center of the thorax from above. The pin should protrude about 8 millimeters ($\frac{1}{2}$ inch) above the body of the specimen. This provides ample room to grasp the pin should the specimen need to be removed from the collection box. It also provides enough room between the body and the bottom of the box to place a label. A pinning board, such as one used to spread the wings of butterflies, may be used for pinning dragonflies, but it is not really necessary unless exact arrangement of the wings is needed. If a pinning board is used, the dragonfly should be left to dry for several days.

The label beneath the specimen should contain the following information:

Date of collection
State and county (or parish) where it was collected
City or nearest identifiable landmark
Collector's name

If desired, a second label with additional habitat and environmental information or species identification can be put below the first label. Otherwise, this information should be kept in a notebook.

Because of their large wings, pinned dragonflies, like pinned butterflies and moths, take up a huge amount of space in a collecting box. To save space, pinned specimens can be shingled; that is, tilted to the side with the right wing higher than the left, overlapping the left wing of the adjacent specimen. Although pinned butterflies and moths are somewhat fragile, they are not nearly as easily broken as pinned dragonflies. Special care must be taken when handling a box of pinned dragonflies; the slightest bump can cause damage to the specimens. Careful treatment is particularly important when a shingled dragonfly is extracted from or placed into the collection box.

Protecting Stored Specimens

Whether pinned or in envelopes, preserved dragonflies must be protected against foraging pests, especially dermestid beetles. Most storage boxes for pinned specimens have tight fitting lids, but this is seldom enough. Napthalene or paradichlorbenzene mothballs or crystals in a small container should be put into every collection box and examined periodically. If you cannot smell it when the box is opened, it needs recharging. Collectors argue about the merits of napthalene over paradichlorbenzene mothballs, but both are effective in keeping the collection safe. The odor of the mothballs or moth crystals is not particularly pleasant. To ensure that it does not permeate your living quarters, the collection should be kept sealed. This alone will help reduce the number of insect invaders.

Collecting Larvae

Collecting dragonfly larvae is much more straightforward than collecting adults. Larvae rely on stealth and camouflage for protection rather than vision and speed, so the collector is not very often engaged in a battle of wits. You will find larvae nearly anywhere a body of water has been present for several weeks. Ponds and small pools are likely to contain members of the Libellulidae (skimmers), Gomphidae (clubtails), and Corduliidae (emeralds) families, while streams and rivers may contain these plus Aeshnidae (darners) and Macromiidae (cruisers) species. Petalurids are a special case, as are the Cordulegastridae (spiketails), because the larvae are restricted to rather specialized aquatic habitats, such as seeps in deeply wooded areas.

Dragonfly larvae may best be located in areas where adults occur. One advantage to collecting larvae is that they are present nearly year-round, especially in the southern part of the country. Cloudy days, rain, cool fronts, and other weather likely to clear the skies of adults will still allow collecting of their larval offspring.

Catching larvae normally requires a net, a sorting pan in which to dump and identify the net's contents, and containers to transport the larvae. Ideally, the net should have sides made of canvas or some other tough material, and the frame should be flat-bottomed and shaped like the letter D. This makes the net easy to sweep across a pond bottom or through aquatic vegetation. The larvae can be extremely small, so the bottom mesh should be fairly fine.

Larvae live in a number of habitats but primarily in shallow water and near banks. Algal mats or other vegetation within a meter (more or less one yard) or so of the shoreline are particularly good places to check for larvae because the vegetation not only provides a place for the larvae to hide from predators but also contains an ample supply of small organisms for them to eat.

After filling the net, dump the contents into the sorting pan. Pans with white bottoms are best because it is easier to see the animals against this background. If needed, add some pond water to the sorting pan and wait for the mud to settle, which should not take long except with the muddiest of water. Then sort though the material in the pan with a white plastic spoon or other utensil and watch for movement. Ponds are usually alive with small animals, and it may take a few moments to see the larvae. While sorting, be careful not to inadvertently handle any creature that you cannot identify.

If you need some help separating dragonfly larvae from other aquatic insects, get a copy of *An Introduction to the Aquatic Insects of North America* edited by Richard Merritt and Kenneth Cummins. Depending on where you are, giant water bugs, backswimmers, and water scorpions may appear in your net and sorting pan. The large *Lethocerus* water bug (also called the electric light bug) is reputed to inflict one of the most painful bites of any insect. Other biting creatures include hellgrammites and beetle larvae. As long as you do not sort with your bare fingers in murky water or work carelessly, they should not cause any difficulty. Water boatmen, which resemble backswimmers, are common but harmless. The best course of action is not to handle any of the collected animals until you know their identities.

None of these aquatic insects are known to be poisonous to the extent of a black widow or brown recluse spider, but be alert for possible allergic reactions to any bite or sting.

Dragonfly larvae can range in size from microscopic, when they are hatchlings, to over 50 millimeters (2 inches) long. Most are drab in color since they rely on camouflage for protection against other predators. Once spotted, they should be placed into a container filled with clean pond water. Several larvae can remain temporarily in a single container, provided they are very close to the same size. Dragonfly larvae are voracious predators and may quickly recover their composure and devour a neighbor, especially one smaller than themselves. Small species, such as the Eastern Amberwing (*Perithemis tenera*), produce smaller larvae, and large species, such as the Widow Skimmer (*Libellula luctuosa*) produce larger larvae. You can determine the relative age of the larvae, no matter what the size, by looking at the wing pads along the back. As a rule, the closer the tips of the wing pads are to the center of the back, the older the larva and the sooner it will emerge as an adult.

Some people also use "string traps" or "rag dolls" to collect larvae. To construct a string trap, make a bundle of 35 to 40 strands of baling twine, each about 1.5 meters (about 5 feet) in length, folded in the middle. Tie the bundle tightly together at about 8 to 10 centimeters (3 to 4 inches) below the fold so that it looks like a rag doll or mop consisting of some 70 to 80 strands of twine. Add a small weight to the loose end of one of the strands and a retrieval line to the assembly at the fold. Throw the entire apparatus out into the water. After a period of several days, slowly retrieve it. Place it in a bucket of water and shake it vigorously to dislodge any occupants, some of which will likely be dragonfly larvae. The trap can then be put back into the water until the next sampling. Like aquatic vegetation, a string trap provides a good hiding place for larvae and a food supply.

Collecting dragonfly larvae directly by picking them up is not as effective as using a net or a string trap. But it may be the only effective method of catching larvae of species such as the Cyrano Darner (*Nasiaeschna pentacantha*). We have collected several larvae of this species from under or in the cracks of loose bark on driftwood or submerged logs. When we remove a piece of driftwood or a log from the water for examination, we make sure to return it back to the water to serve as a home for more animals.

Once the larvae are in transfer containers, they should be kept cool and out of direct sunlight. A small ice chest is ideal. The water should not need aeration for quite some time if it is reasonably cool and the dragonflies are not overcrowded.

Preserving Larvae

Larval collections are best kept in small glass vials of about 15 to 20 milliliters ($\frac{1}{2}$ to $\frac{3}{4}$ ounce). The vials may then be put in boxes containing subdivided inserts or in vial racks. To preserve the larvae, either place them directly into the preservative or put them in the freezer before preserving. The preservative may be one of several available. The simplest is 70 percent isopropanol, sold as rubbing alcohol in stores. Using a mixture of ten parts alcohol and one part glycerin has several advantages. First, specimens will not be as

brittle as with alcohol alone. Second, if the alcohol part of the solution in the vial dries out, the specimen will not be ruined because the glycerin will help keep it hydrated. Even though you can buy absolute alcohol (100 percent), do not use greater concentrations than 70 to 75 percent. Conversely, do not use a concentration of less than about 60 percent. If the alcohol is not concentrated enough, the specimens will deteriorate. Some collectors add one-half part glacial acetic acid to the preservative to serve as a rapidly penetrating fixative, but for most collections this is not necessary.

Unlike adult dragonfly collections, other insects are not a danger to larval collections. The biggest hazard is desiccation of the preservative because of loose-fitting lids. While many vials are sold with screw caps and sealing liners, over time there is still loss of the preservative. We prefer tight-fitting rubber stoppers for maintaining the integrity of the seal for a longer period, even though they are less aesthetic and much bulkier in the collection.

Each vial should have a label with the same information on it as for adults.

{ FIGURE 94 }

The Mantled Baskettail (Epitheca semiaquea), *a species of the eastern United States. Before collecting this species, or any other dragonfly, review the DSA Collecting Statement [see Appendix C/ pages 213-14]. Photo © Robert A. Behrstock/Naturewide Images.*

With larval collections, detailed habitat data are even more important. Adults are mobile and may move long distances if the local environment is not suitable. Larvae are more susceptible to their surroundings, and information on their habitat is more relevant to the ecology of each species. Since the labels are by necessity very small, we recommend that you also maintain a journal that records pertinent information about each larva or group of larvae collected.

Collecting and Preserving Exuviae

When larvae molt into adults, the skin from the last larval stage, the exuvia, remains behind. Almost all of the physical details from the larva remain, and the skin may be used, in most instances, to identify the dragonfly species. If placed in water or one of the preservatives mentioned above, exuviae will become pliable. Key characteristics such as spines and mouthparts can easily be seen and in some cases pulled into viewable position with little effort [see Figure 25]. An interested collector can find exuviae near most fresh water, especially on reeds, cattails, dock piers, tree trunks, rocks, or snags that are in the water or close to the water's edge. The legs of the exuviae are usually firmly attached to whatever the structure, and special care should

be taken to remove it from its perch without damage. Dried exuviae are extremely brittle and should be put into a vial of preservative as soon as possible.

Think before Collecting

While dragonflies are generally suited to the traditional collecting and museum curating methods that work so well with other insects, their special requirements should be soberly considered before starting a collection [Figure 94]. This is a serious undertaking, but with care and commitment, a properly maintained collection can be a source of valuable information and much pleasure.

CHAPTER EIGHT

WATER GARDENING
FOR DRAGONFLIES

Dragonflies are strong fliers, but sometimes they are whisked away by breezes and weather fronts and scattered to the winds. Their adventures carry them to many far-off places, but on their journeys they may pause for a short time in your yard. The more agreeable the environment, the more likely they are to stay for a while. Just as people plant a "butterfly garden" to attract butterflies, you can attract passing dragonflies (and damselflies) by adding a pond or water feature—a "dragonfly garden"—to your property. Many popular books and websites go into far more detail about the design and construction of water gardens than is possible here, but a few simple pond plans will serve our purpose.

We once tried to determine the smallest pool or water garden that would attract dragonflies during a study on the use of constructed wetlands for control of agricultural pollution. We created a series of experimental "ponds" that consisted simply of square holes dug into the ground and lined with heavy plastic. The ponds ranged in size from 30 centimeters (about 1 foot) square to 122 centimeters (4 feet) square and were dug to a depth of roughly 100 centimeters (3 feet). Approximately 15 centimeters (6 inches) of soil was placed on the bottom of each pond, and water depth was maintained at about 30 centimeters (12 inches) for the duration of the study.

Half of the ponds were planted with cattail that grew to a height of almost 2 meters (6 feet), and half were planted with a low-growing sedge that projected 15 to 30 centimeters (6 to 12 inches) above the water's surface. While these ponds were not particularly aesthetic, all of them attracted dragonfly and damselfly adults, and the dragonflies laid eggs in all but the smallest pond.

During the summer of 2002, we helped conduct another study to evaluate whether commercially available aquatic dyes prevented dragonflies, particularly Wandering Gliders (*Pantala flavescens*), from laying eggs into

{FIGURE 95}

A female American Rubyspot damselfly
(Hetaerina americana).
Photo © James L. Lasswell.

{ FIGURE 96 }

A garden waterfall at Grape Creek Country Market east of Fredricksburg, Texas. The running water, with plenty of vegetation to perch on nearby, provides an excellent habitat for several dragonfly and damselfly species. Photo © Jack Brady.

a body of water. The study was carried out in a series of twelve aluminum cattle watering troughs. Each trough was roughly 4 meters (12 feet) long, 60 centimeters (2 feet) wide, and 75 centimeters (2.5 feet) deep. A layer of soil approximately 15 centimeters (6 inches) was spread across the bottom of each trough and water was added to within 10 centimeters (4 inches) of the top. No plants were placed into the troughs.

The dye—the same kind used to help prevent algal growth in golf course ponds—was added to three troughs at the recommended rate, to three troughs at three times the recommended rate, and to another three troughs at six times the recommended rate. Three troughs contained only water.

Within thirty days, adult Wandering Gliders began to emerge and eventually appeared at all twelve study troughs.

{ F I G U R E   9 7 }

When this photo was taken at Grape Creek Country Market east of Fredericksburg, Texas, two damselfly and three dragonfly species were at the pool. Photo © Jack Brady.

Wandering Gliders typically lay their eggs in temporary pools, so the larvae must develop rapidly. Thirty days, however, was much faster than we expected in this situation. It seemed remarkable that in a trough containing only soil and water a carnivorous dragonfly larva could find enough food to develop into an adult. The artificial ponds become small ecosystems and, like islands in an ocean, these reservoirs are quickly colonized by a surprisingly large number of organisms. Algae grew almost immediately with the soil providing dissolved nutrients to promote its growth. Water boatmen and water beetles appeared soon after the troughs were filled with water, bringing with them attached spores, cells, and microbes to inoculate the new pond. Midges were also quick to appear and lay eggs, as were some mosquitoes. Mayflies found these small bodies of water and soon their larvae were established. The predatory backswimmers and big water bugs eventually showed up, and before long, the seemingly barren pools became thriving microcosms of aquatic life.

Attracting Dragonflies to Your Water Garden

Attracting dragonflies to your pond or water garden is not difficult. In fact, it would be practically impossible to keep them out. The experimental ponds described above illustrate how little is needed to induce dragonflies to lay eggs. With just a little more effort, you should be able to attract a broad range of species and persuade them to linger in your garden.

As with buying a new home, location is everything. The experimental troughs were in an open, sunny locality that received no shade during the day. In addition, there were no tall plants in or near the water for perching and little nearby cover. The adults generally paused just long enough to lay eggs and then moved on. In the study where we constructed in-ground ponds, several large ponds nearby helped attract a greater number and diversity of dragonflies than we saw at or near the troughs.

Adult dragonflies and damselflies are very mobile insects. The probability is quite high that virtually every species in your area will come by your yard at some time during the course of a couple of years. But what makes them stay? Some species will be hard to draw in no matter what. The river cruisers (genus *Macromia*) prefer long stretches of flowing water and are seldom found anywhere except rivers. The broad-winged damselflies (family Calopterygidae) also prefer flowing water. At least one species in this family, the American Rubyspot (*Hetaerina americana*), will come to small fountains [Figure 95]. If a water garden has flowing water in addition to a still pool, it will be more likely to attract a large range of both dragonfly and damselfly species [Figures 96, 97].

Sunny Is Better

Many dragonflies and damselflies will forage or seek shelter in shaded woods, but most prefer a sunny open spot to find a mate and lay eggs. The most common group of dragonflies drawn to water gardens, the skimmers

{FIGURE 98}

A majestic male Great Blue Skimmer (Libellula vibrans), *a resident of much of the southeastern and eastern United States. Scan provided by authors.*

(family Libellulidae), generally prefers ponds that are sunny to partly sunny. The Great Blue Skimmer (*Libellula vibrans*) [*Figure 98*], the Slaty Skimmer (*Libellula incesta*) [*Figure 99*], and the Neon Skimmer (*Libellula croceipennis*) [see Figures 1, 19], however, do quite well along shady stretches of streams and shady ponds. During the summer months, the Slaty Skimmer and Neon Skimmer are quite numerous at a golf course near Weatherford, Texas. Several $\frac{1}{2}$ to 1 hectare (1 to 2.5 acres) ponds are on the course, and water flows from the upper ponds to the lower ones through a dense stand of oak and willow. The woods at this location draw the highest number of Slaty and Neon Skimmers. On occasion we have found them perched in the sun just outside the wooded areas, but when disturbed they normally fly straight back into the woods.

The dragonfly species found at the open, sunny ponds include species such as the Sulphur-tipped Clubtail (*Gomphus militaris*) [*Figure 100*], Flag-tailed Spinyleg

{FIGURE 99}

The wings of the male Slaty Skimmer (Libellula incesta) *Skimmer's are completely clear.*
This dragonfly's range is much the same as the Great Blue Skimmer's. Photo © Greg W. Lasley.

(*Dromogomphus spoliatus*) *[Figure 101]*, and Common Green Darner (*Anax junius*) [see Figures 20, 53, 54]. But the most common species were skimmers. The Common Whitetail (*Libellula lydia*) [see Figures 47, 48, 49], Widow Skimmer (*Libellula luctuosa*) [see Figure 58], Eastern Pondhawk (*Erythemis simplicicollis*) *[Figure 102]*, Swift Setwing (*Dythemis velox*) *[Figure 103]*, Checkered Setwing (*Dythemis fugax*) *[Figure 104]*, Black Saddlebags (*Tramea lacerata*) [see Figures 55, 56], Red Saddlebags (*Tramea onusta*), Halloween Pennant (*Celithemis eponina*) *[Figures 105, 106]*, and the small, but colorful Eastern Amberwing (*Perithemis tenera*) [see Figure 45] were all quite numerous.

When females are near a pond, they spend much of their time avoiding males, mating, or laying eggs, often with a male in attendance or even still attached in the tandem position. Few males, however, will pursue females away from the pond into a wooded or sheltered area and risk losing their patrol station to a competitor.

Pond Size and Aquatic Vegetation

The larger the pond, the more dragonfly species it is likely to attract and support. Dragonflies also seem to respond to the presence of emergent vegetation—plants rooted in the water but with most of their growth above it—around the pond. The plants serve as resting or perching places for males as they survey their territory for food, possible mates, or the incursion of another male. Emergent vegetation also provides an excellent place for larvae to crawl upon to molt into adults.

Ponds with a significant amount of submerged vegetation seem to support more species of dragonflies than those with emergent vegetation alone. Species such as the Halloween Pennant, Calico Pennant (*Celithemis elisa*) *[Figure 107]*, Banded Pennant (*Celithemis fasciata*) *[Figure 108]*, and both species of setwings [see Figures 103, 104] frequent these types of ponds, sometimes in fairly large numbers. The submerged vegetation surely offers convenient hiding places for the small larvae of these species.

Bottom Type

The type of bottom in the pond also helps determine which larvae will survive. The larvae of many species of skimmers will be at home on a sandy or rocky bottom,

{FIGURE 100}

The Sulphur-tipped Clubtail (Gomphus militaris) *is a common sight at lakes, ponds, and slow-moving streams and rivers from Texas northward into Nebraska. Photo © Greg W. Lasley.*

{FIGURE 101}

The Flag-tailed Spinyleg (Dromogomphus spoliatus) *visits lakes, ponds, and slow-moving streams and rivers from Texas north into Canada. Scan provided by authors.*

The mature male Eastern Pondhawk
(Erythemis simplicicollis) is soft blue in color
but with a green face and white "cerci" –
appendages at the tip of the abdomen. The
Eastern Pondhawk frequents ponds, lakes,
and slow-moving rivers and streams. Scan
provided by authors.

especially in shallow water. Most of the clubtails, however, prefer a soft mud bottom because the larvae remain buried or partially buried until it is time for them to emerge as adults.

Water Filtration

Filtration is an important asset to small pond maintenance in the water garden but needs to be approached with care for dragonfly and damselfly larvae to thrive. Freshly hatched larvae are miniscule, almost microscopic. Since most pump and filter combinations sit on the bottom of the pond, the larvae can easily be sucked into the filtration unit and killed. An easy way to avoid this problem is to elevate the pump and filter off the bottom on bricks or rocks. Although not a perfect solution, the in-flow to the filter will be less brisk at the bottom of the pond and less of a danger to the larvae crawling about.

Small Backyard Water Gardens

Ponds and water gardens are as varied as the people who build them, and personal selections of rocks, bottom types, pumps, filters, plants, and fish ensure that no two will be exactly alike.

{ F I G U R E   103 }

The Swift Setwing (Dythemis velox) *has brown wingtips and usually perches with its wings slanted downward. The setwing in this photo has its abdomen raised in a behavior called "obelisking." This behavior, often seen on warm days, helps decrease the amount of body surface exposed to the sun, thus reducing the dragonfly's body temperature. Photo © James L. Lasswell.*

One of us maintains four small water gardens in the backyard of his central Texas home. The largest of these is constructed of landscape timbers that support a thick rubber liner (45-mil). It is about 1.2 meters (4 feet) by 2.4 meters (8 feet) and holds about 950 liters (250 gallons) of water. The bottom is composed of pea gravel, and the aquatic plants are growing in pots placed on the bottom, put on

{F I G U R E 104, *below*}

A male Checkered Setwing (Dythemis fugax) is readily recognized by the lacy brown pattern at the base of the wings. Scan provided by authors.

{F I G U R E 105}

It is easy to see why this beautifully colored male dragonfly has been given the name Halloween Pennant (Celithemis eponina). Its range extends throughout the eastern half of the United States and north into Canada. Scan provided by authors.

{F I G U R E 106, *top right*}

The female Halloween Pennant (Celithemis eponina) is marked in much the same way as the male, but the wings are not as deep orange. Scan provided by authors.

This brightly colored small dragonfly is a male Calico Pennant (Celithemis elisa). *Note the red heart-shaped spots on the top of the abdomen. Photo © Curtis E. Williams.*

stands, or suspended from the side. These include rushes, water lilies, dwarf bamboo, water penny, and lizard tail. A few goldfish live in the pond, and in summer, mollies (genus *Poecilia*) are added. The in-pond pump and filter unit is attached to a ground fault interrupt-protected circuit, and water circulates via a small fountain head at one end. Several species of dragonflies frequent the pond, including the Neon Skimmer, Common Whitetail, Eastern Pondhawk, Black Saddlebags, Common Green Darner, and Spot-winged Glider. Desert Firetails (*Telebasis salva*) are the most common damselfly visitors, and six or seven of the bright red

{FIGURE 108}

The Banded Pennant (Celithemis fasciata) *often associates with both the Halloween Pennant and Calico Pennant. Photo © Robert A. Behrstock/Naturewide Images.*

males are usually flying in the vicinity [Figure 109].

A second water garden consists of a 570-liter (150-gallon) plastic watering trough normally used for livestock [Figure 110]. It also has a gravel bottom and the same pump-filter-fountain head combination. Water lilies, parrot feather, water penny, and water iris grow in this pond, all in pots that sit either on the bottom or on stands. The pond also contains some small goldfish and mollies. This garden sits in a shady cul-de-sac between the side of the house and a tall, wooden fence. It still attracts Neon Skimmers and Eastern Pondhawks and an occasional Swift Setwing, such as one that

was perched atop a twig just a meter (3 feet) or so away from the pool [Figure 111]. One day as the pond was being cleaned a Common Green Darner larva turned up [see Figure 81], although its parents had not been seen at or near the pond. The larva was living in an overturned strawberry planter that was being used as a plant stand. Since the larva was quite large, it had been there for a while, successfully avoiding both the goldfish and the mollies.

The third water garden is a small, commercially produced model with a wooden frame that hides the 190-liter (50-gallon) plastic tub holding the water. It has a gravel bottom, no fish, a small water lily at one end, and a dwarf cattail that escaped from its pot and is growing rampant in the bottom. The cattail makes it difficult for dragonflies to maneuver their way to the water, though

{FIGURE 109}

A male Desert Firetail (Telebasis salva), *a damselfly, on a blade of grass. These are common inhabitants of water gardens in the southwestern United States. Photo © James L. Lasswell.*

Neon Skimmers still try. Damselflies, however, such as small bluets (genus *Enallagma*) [Figure 112] and Desert Firetails, have no trouble negotiating the stems.

The fourth water garden is a small waterfall in the corner of a deck. A concrete bowl, about 75 centimeters (30 inches) across, sits at the bottom of the waterfall on a concrete pedestal and holds 76 liters (20 gallons) of water. A small pump circulates the water to the top of a 45-centimeter-high run (18 inches), where it trickles and splashes back down into the bowl. Large river rocks lie in the bottom of the bowl and water mint grows around its edge. A pot of frogfruit (*Phyla incisa*) dug from the yard is sometimes wedged into the bottom rocks. The running water has attracted an American Rubyspot damselfly on more than one occasion, and in 2001, eleven Spot-winged Gliders emerged into adults over the course of the summer, their exuviae left as souvenirs on the side of the concrete bowl.

The dragonflies attracted to these ponds only stay for a day or so. Generally, they do not perch on the pond vegetation but near the pond, on flower stalks or plant

{FIGURE 110}

This small 570-liter (150-gallon) water garden attracts a number of different dragonfly and damselfly species. Photo © Forrest L. Mitchell.

supports. While the individual ponds are too small for a male dragonfly to establish and patrol a territory, male Neon Skimmers have turned all four ponds into one big water garden, patrolling each of the four in turn.

Fish

In nature, dragonflies cope with most other pond and wetland species. The backyard water garden, however, is normally an artificial habitat, and you need to take this into consideration if you wish to have dragon-flies as permanent summer tenants. The major predators of dragonfly and damselfly larvae are probably fish. To coexist, larvae have evolved protective coloring and stealthy habits, but a pond full of fish will eliminate a large number of larvae if they are not given cover. The protection of dense vegetation and shallow water can help. Keeping small fish can, too. Goldfish are a problem because they often feed on the bottom, and dragonfly larvae hiding in the mud can easily become part of a hungry goldfish's evening meal.

One fish species to avoid, especially in small water gardens, is the mosquito fish (*Gambusia affinis*). Mosquito fish are excellent candidates for a water garden unless you are trying to raise dragonflies. They readily adapt to just about any aquatic habitat; they are extremely prolific; they really do eat mosquitoes; and they overwinter (at least in the southern United States) without any problem. They are also particularly adept and insatiable predators that eat everything they can catch, including dragonfly eggs and larvae.

In the water gardens described above, mollies have been reasonably compatible.

{ F I G U R E 111 }

The Swift Setwing (Dythemis velox) *near one of four backyard water gardens. Photo © Forrest L. Mitchell.*

While they will eat invertebrates and smaller fish, they are more vegetarian than goldfish and spend much of their time eating unwanted algae. They are less prone to forage on the bottom of the pond, spending most of their time at the top, along the sides, or in the vegetation. Sailfin mollies (*Poecilia latipinna*) are especially colorful inhabitants, but in cool climates all mollies must be brought inside to an aquarium during the winter, since they cannot survive extended chilling. People usually want

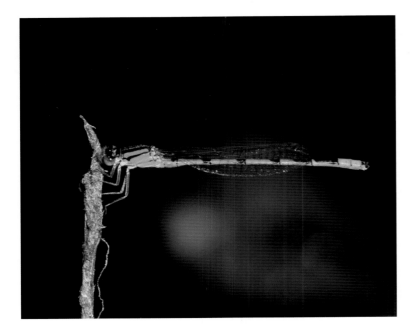

A frequent visitor to water gardens is the Familiar Bluet damselfly (Enallagma civile). *Photo © James L. Lasswell.*

to have fish in their water gardens, but if they also want to have dragonflies, they have to choose the fish wisely.

Relax and Observe

Small water gardens are definitely attractive and colorful additions to any backyard, much like a bed of roses or a planting of multicolored caladiums. Many people build larger, more elaborate water gardens that often serve as the focal point of their outdoor activities at home. A couple of large shade trees, a miniature waterfall, rock-strewn streams, bridges, colorful aquatic and terrestrial plants, and a large pool filled with brightly colored fish make a pleasing place to sit back and relax after a hard day's work (or play).

In either situation, you will enjoy adult dragonflies and damselflies, but you will have to watch much more closely to see the aquatic stages of these insects. With patience, you may get to see a dragonfly larva crawl out of the water and emerge as an adult during the course of an evening. It never ceases to amaze us that these ugly, fierce-looking creatures can crawl out of the water onto dry land and turn into beautiful, brightly colored, flying insects.

Rearing Dragonflies

In chapter four, we discussed the stages of growth a dragonfly larva goes through after hatching from an egg. While this is relatively interesting to read about, it is much more fun to observe. You can easily do this by collecting a few larvae from a local pond or stream or from your backyard water garden and raising them yourself.

Although some dragonfly larvae are active hunters, most are sedentary, spending their time buried in mud or hiding in algal mats or other vegetation. The skimmers [Figure 113] and green darners are mostly hide-and-ambush predators and are good candidates to be raised in captivity. The larvae of the Common Green Darner, much like tropical fish, become so used to being fed that they will rush to the side of their aquarium at feeding time. Clubtails [see Figure 77], however, are burrowers, and when placed into an aquarium with a mud or sand bottom will spend much of the time hidden from sight. Obviously, this makes them harder to observe and more difficult to feed than skimmers or green darners.

The following discussion pertains mostly to skimmers and green darners because of their wide range, relative ease of capture, and amenability to rearing in an aquarium. Summer and fall are good times to collect dragonfly larvae, although they can be collected year-round if the water body is not frozen or icebound. (See Chapter 7 for details on collecting larvae.)

Aquariums for Rearing

A full-sized fish tank is not necessary for rearing dragonfly larvae; the smaller the container, the easier it is to clean and to observe the larvae. Containers for this purpose do not have to be elaborate or expensive [Figure 114]. They can be constructed, bought from discount stores, or salvaged from materials found around the house, but they do need to be clean and free from soap or cleansers.

We have reared a number of larvae in plastic petri dishes that measured only 15 centimeters (6 inches) across and about 2.5 centimeters (1 inch) deep. A single larva was raised in each dish with only a sand bottom and a small piece of plastic aquarium plant for it to hide under and crawl onto when ready to emerge. Plastic soft drink bottles can be cut to size. Small plastic food containers also work well, although many have opaque sides so their contents can be viewed only from above. Inexpensive glass bowls are a good choice in situations where breakage will not be a problem, as with children and indoor pets. Cats, especially, are inveterate naturalists and will certainly want to assist with any project involving bowls of water and small animals.

{FIGURE 113}

Larval Twelve-spotted Skimmer (Libellula pulchella) *in a laboratory rearing container. Photo © James L. Lasswell.*

Many shops now carry small hexagonal plastic containers meant to display Siamese fighting fish (*Betta splendens*) and these are also useful for rearing dragonfly larvae. Goldfish bowls that close in at the top are not a good choice because the emerging adult may be trapped inside and fall back into the water, where it will drown.

Our favorite containers for rearing dragonfly larvae are 20 to 25 centimeters (8 to 10 inches) in diameter, 6 to 8 centimeters (2 to 3 inches) deep and have straight, smooth sides so that the larvae cannot crawl out. The advantage of such a container is that it allows room for small

rocks and pieces of plastic aquarium plants. It also allows for easy viewing of the contents from the top and, with the right combination and placement of rocks and vegetation, it can be an aesthetically pleasing place to raise dragonfly larvae.

Water Supply

The kind of water in the aquarium is important. Chlorinated or otherwise treated municipal water supplies are toxic to the larvae unless treated to remove the chlorine and chloramines that may be present. Many commercial products are sold for this purpose in the tropical fish trade and should be readily available. Products that contain a substance called stress coat or any aloe vera derivatives are not necessary. Unlike fish, dragonfly larvae do not have protective slime layers that need replenishing. Water treated with in-home water softeners is also detrimental because it contains added sodium.

Bottled spring water sold in stores by the gallon is a good choice for rearing larvae. It is inexpensive, has been heavily filtered, and contains no chemical sterilizing agents. Pond water from where the larva was collected

{ f I G U R E 114 }

Containers used for rearing dragonfly larvae. Photo © James L. Lasswell.

is also usually fine to use, but it sometimes contains pollutants that can get concentrated as the water evaporates from the aquarium and may eventually kill the larvae.

Never use distilled or reverse-osmosis prepared water for any aquatic animal. This water is lethal to aquatic life since it has no dissolved elements or other buffers to protect the animal from an osmotic imbalance. Freshwater insects are generally hyperosmotic to their environment,

meaning they have higher ion and amino acid concentrations than the water surrounding them. Dragonfly larvae and other insect larvae that live in fresh water are generally quite permeable to water, which diffuses into and out of them. In distilled water, the flow becomes one way and the insect must expend a lot of energy trying to rid its body of excess water. If it cannot keep up, its cells in effect become waterlogged and it dies.

In addition to a good water supply, dragonfly larvae also need something on the bottom of the aquarium to burrow into. Thoroughly washed sand has the advantage of being light colored, making the larvae more visible against the background. It also supports plastic plants or twigs for the larvae to crawl onto before emerging as adults. The fine grains are suitable for small containers, and food stays on the surface where the larvae can see it. Aquarium gravel is also appropriate, and it comes in various sizes and grades as well as in a selection of colors. Mud or clay bottoms function well and may be preferable for burrowing species such as clubtails. They are more difficult to clean and, if disturbed, may make the water muddy.

Food and Feeding

Dragonfly larvae require live food. They will typically eat anything that is moving and small enough to catch, except after they are first transferred from their natural habitat into the aquarium, when they may not eat anything. The length of this adjustment period varies from one larva to another, even within the same species, and may last from a few minutes to a day or more.

If the pond or stream where you collected your larvae is nearby and not frozen over, it will probably provide an abundant source of food. Nearly any small, swimming creature will do—water fleas, scuds, mayfly larvae, bloodworms, midge larvae, mosquito larvae. It does not really matter which of these organisms you feed to the larvae; if it is the right size and moves, drop it in the aquarium. If the larva wants it, it will eat it. Enough food can often be collected in a single trip to supply the larvae for a week or more.

Another place to get food is an aquarium store or pet store that sells tropical fish. These may stock water fleas (*Daphnia*), white worms (Enchytraeidae), black worms (*Tubifex*), mealworms (*Tenebrio*), wingless fruit flies (*Drosophila*), and newborn guppies or mosquito fish.

Choosing what to feed the larvae will depend on their size. Small specimens can eat water fleas, wingless fruit flies (both the adults and the larvae), and white worms. Larger specimens may accept the other selections, and the very largest will likely eat small fish. The fact that many of these fish foods are terrestrial (white worms, mealworms, and fruit flies) is of little importance as long as they remain active in the water for a long enough period of time to catch the larva's attention.

Most dragonfly larvae are not good surface feeders; if the water in the aquarium is deep, look for organisms that will readily sink to the bottom. Some of the foods listed above will float, and unless the water is shallow, as in a small bowl or petri dish, the larvae will not be able to grab them off the surface. A really good source of food for shallow water feeding is mosquito larvae, which are usually plentiful in most areas of the world during warm weather. Since it is the habit of both the larvae and the pupae (the tumblers) to float on the surface when undisturbed, the water must be shallow enough for the dragonfly larvae to reach them from the bottom.

Another option is to rear a food supply for the larvae. We have raised larvae on a diet consisting mainly of white worms, which are easily kept. Supply houses sell starter cultures of white worms, and many advertise in the classified ads of aquarium and tropical fish magazines. The same is true of water fleas and wingless fruit flies. You can also collect mosquito larvae. Fill a pan with water, add some dried leaves and a little potting soil, and put it in a secluded spot. If you keep the pan filled, the resulting supply of mosquito larvae, at least in warm weather, will help supplement your larvae's diet.

Larvae may be fed daily or every other day and, if necessary, may go for a weekend without being fed. Variety helps when planning the larval diet; they seem to get tired of eating the same fare. For the most part, you can leave aquatic animals in the aquarium for the larvae to feed on at will. Uneaten aquatic insect larvae, such as mosquitoes, however, should be removed to prevent them from emerging in the house. White worms, mealworms, wingless fruit flies, and other terrestrial food items should also be removed if not eaten in a short period of time to prevent them from decaying and fouling the water.

Determine the amount of food you give by how much the larvae can eat in twenty to thirty minutes. Remember that as a larva gets older it will need more food. It will also

{ F I G U R E 115 }

A newly emerged saddlebags that had been housed in a laboratory beaker. Note that the larva crawled to the top of the twig outside the beaker before the adult emerged. Had it only crawled halfway, or had the twig been too short, it could have been trapped between the twig and the jar and not been able to properly expand its wings. Photo © Larissa Heimer.

excrete more and may contaminate the water more quickly. The water should be changed anytime it becomes foul, whether by the larvae or by the food source. You can use an inexpensive turkey baster to remove the water without disturbing the larvae. Bigger larvae (provided they are not newly molted) are sturdy enough to be plucked out and put in a bowl while their habitat is being cleaned.

Adult Emergence

When a larva reaches the stage where it is about ready to emerge as an adult dragonfly, it will suddenly quit eating. At this time, some changes have taken place inside its exoskeleton that are not readily seen. As with all its other molts (see Chapter 4), a fresh, delicate exoskeleton is formed inside the one that is to be cast off. When this has happened, the head and eyes of the soon-to-be-new dragonfly separate ever so slightly from the old outer skin. The eyes of the larva, within a day or so, take on a dead, opaque look for they no longer serve as an organ of vision for the future adult dragonfly still encased inside. When it reaches this stage, make sure it has something to crawl out on and then just leave it alone and let nature take its course.

The process of emergence is an extremely critical stage in the life of a dragonfly, and any disruption whatsoever can damage or kill the larva or teneral dragonfly. If, after coming out of the water, the larva falls back into the water it will normally make another attempt. If it does not find a suitable place to latch on to, it will die. Once the larva comes out of the water, leave it alone. It is all right to take pictures and admire it, but do not touch it and do not pick it up. This will often stress the larva enough that the adult will not emerge, and it will die within a short period of time.

The plant or other structure put into the aquarium for emergence should be placed so that the dragonfly has ample room to complete its transformation. In an open container, such as a bowl, this should not be a problem since the platform may be a rock or a twig projecting at a very shallow angle with no space where the larva might become trapped. With narrow, deep containers, such as Siamese fighting fish tanks, raise the water level so that the larva is forced up and out of the tank.

A teneral dragonfly is extremely delicate and should be left alone until it has had time to expand its wings and abdomen [*Figure 115*]. It should also remain untouched until it has hardened.

Rearing Dragonflies: A Long-term Commitment?

Rearing a larva to the adult stage usually requires a long-term commitment. Most of the species caught in small ponds will emerge within the year, and the larger the larva the sooner it will become an adult. Sometimes even large larvae can take their time developing. We once captured a half-grown larva of a Cyrano Darner that spent two years living in an aquarium before surprising the staff by flying through the laboratory as they walked in one morning.

The great thing about rearing dragonflies is that once they have reached maturity you can take them out and release them. You have helped produce a new generation of dragonflies for all of us to watch and enjoy.

PICTURING
DRAGONFLIES

Nearly all entomologists have, at one time or another, made an insect collection. For many of us, collecting came first and led us into the profession of entomology. A lot has been written about the joys (or evils) of collecting, and it is an important facet of entomology.

Some insects, although beautiful in life, lose much of their color when captured, preserved, and added to a collection. No group of insects can be more frustrating in this regard than the dragonflies and damselflies. In life, they rival any insect for color. In collections, they become dull, easily broken, and difficult to maintain. As a result, a growing number of professional entomologists and amateur naturalists alike now seek to capture and preserve the beautiful shapes and colors of these large insects through photography or computer scanning. [Figure 116]

The right equipment, experience, and patience make photographs like this of a Faded Pennant (Celithemis ornata) *possible. Photo © James L. Lasswell.*

Not everyone will want to take the time and effort needed for the detailed images of dragonflies that can be obtained by scanning. In fact, many of the naturalists we have met over the past few years at professional entomology meetings or nature festivals around the country, while curious about the scanning procedure, have expressed a greater interest in dragonfly photography. We receive numerous e-mail requests to identify dragonflies from photographs people have taken.

During the 2002 Dragonfly Festival in Roswell, New Mexico, a serious discussion about the best way to photograph dragonflies ended with a participant's tongue-in-cheek observation that "first you need a camera and then you need a dragonfly." He was definitely correct, but you also need information about the camera equipment and field techniques most suited for the purpose.

Photographing Dragonflies

Most photographers try to take good close-up shots of dragonflies for identification purposes. That was our goal when we first started photographing dragonflies in 1994.

It is disappointing when the background of a photograph commands as much attention as the subject. This was, unfortunately, the case with this picture of a Thornbush Dasher (Micrathyria hagenii). *Photo © James L. Lasswell.*

As our collection of dragonfly photos grew, we began to appreciate not only those images that aided identification but also those that were artistic in nature. We now look for opportunities to take both types of photos, and oftentimes a single photo qualifies as both. Many of the photographs published in dragonfly field guides are certainly also works of art.

Since natural-looking shots of dragonflies are difficult if not impossible to pose, most of the opportunities to take either type of photo occur, to a large extent, by happenstance. Studying dragonfly habitats and habits, however, can greatly increase the photographer's chances of obtaining the perfect shot.

There are a number of excellent dragonfly photographers in North America whose dragonfly images appear in a variety of books and websites, including ours. What these individuals have in common is an appreciation of nature and the creatures that live in it. Sort through their photo collections, and you will likely see photos of not only dragonflies but also a host of other animals they had the opportunity to photograph when out in the field. One trip we took to the Big Thicket region of southeast Texas produced photos of several species of dragonflies and damselflies, six different species of swallowtail butterflies, the Red-spotted Purple butterfly (*Limenitis arthemis*), and even a copperhead snake (*Agkistrodon contortrix*) that posed sedately on a warm sandy roadway winding through a thick pine forest. Look for photo opportunities like these; they are absolutely everywhere.

Field Techniques

Although we strive to get quality photos of dragonflies when we are out in the field, we also want to collect images of as many different species as we can, either in the form of photographs or scans (see "Scanning Dragonflies" below). To accomplish this we usually carry both photographic equipment and collecting gear on our outings. We sometimes pass up a photo opportunity in order to collect a specimen for scanning and avoid the chance of it flying away while we are trying to photograph it. For the dedicated photographer, this is sometimes hard to do.

Let us assume that you have chosen to leave the net at home and that you have located a dragonfly you wish to photograph. What do you do then? If all you want is a picture of a dragonfly, you can simply start taking shots as soon as you get close enough to see that it is a dragonfly in your viewfinder. If, however, you want a good close-up or a more artistic shot, there are several things to take into consideration.

If you want a close-up for identification purposes, the background does not make much difference unless it masks identifying characteristics. But background is extremely important for artistic shots. A lot of in-focus clutter immediately behind the

An excellent digital photo of a male Comanche Skimmer (Libellula comanche). *Photo © John C. Seibel/John Seibel Photography.*

dragonfly is a definite distraction *[Figure 117]*. The best backgrounds for any dragonfly photo are those with relatively uniform color, that is, a clay bank, a stand of grass, or even water. The farther the background is behind the subject, the more likely it is to show up in the picture as a pleasing out-of-focus blur of color.

To get an idea of how to accomplish this, look for shots like the one of a male Comanche Skimmer (*Libellula comanche*) *[Figure 118]*. It was taken with ambient light, and the background, located a couple of meters (6 feet) behind the subject, is shallow, clear water with a rough rock bottom. Although this photo was taken without a tripod, you will

{F I G U R E 119}

Halloween Pennant (Celithemis eponina).
Photo © James L. Lasswell.

have more control over your photographs if you use one. A tripod allows for greater leeway on shutter speed and aperture settings. This is true whether or not a flash is used.

Handheld shots restrict the shutter speed and, therefore, also determine somewhat the aperture settings. Here a flash is often desirable to get the depth of field, or range of focus, necessary for a good, detailed photo. Flash photography can create interesting artistic images such as the one of a Halloween Pennant *[Figure 119]*. This photo was taken during the daytime with flash at $^1/_{250}$th second and an f-stop of f-16+.

The resulting photo, with the beautiful orange dragonfly superimposed on the black background, makes for a very striking image.

After planning the type of shot you want, you must then decide whether to photograph the dragonfly from above or from the side. When taking photos for identification purposes, both views are preferable *[Figures 120, 121]*. Sometimes an extremely cooperative dragonfly will seem to want to have its picture taken and photographing both views is no problem. Usually, however, you are lucky to get even a single photo before the subject takes off into the sky.

Terrain and sunlight often determine the angle of approach. Try not to let your shadow fall on the dragonfly. Darners and other species that hang down from their perches are usually best photographed in a vertical format. Horizontally or obliquely perched dragonflies are usually best photographed in a horizontal format. Before approaching, determine which format would be best, then preset the focus to the size of image desired and move the camera into position.

A top view of a Black-tipped Darner (Aeshna tuberculifera). *Photo © Dave Westover.*

Once you begin your approach, move very slowly and avoid sudden or side-to-side movements. Make sure that there are no loose camera straps or anything else that might fall down or move in the wind. Any sudden motion may cause the dragonfly to fly away. As you approach the dragonfly, watch its wings. If they jerk suddenly, it may be a sign that it is getting nervous. Hold still for a few seconds to allow it to settle down, and then renew your approach. Have the camera ready and slow down as you get closer.

Before pressing the shutter, make sure that the plane of the film (or lens in the case of a digital camera) is as parallel to the dragonfly's body as possible. The entire length of the dragonfly, from head to tail, should be in focus. Carefully adjust the camera angle after getting into position. Make sure to take your photos with as small

A side view of a Black-tipped Darner (Aeshna tuberculifera).
Photo © Dave Westover.

an aperture setting as possible, preferably f-16 or smaller. This will give a good depth of field, which is desirable, but sometimes difficult to obtain in close-up photos. If possible, always bracket the shots, that is, vary the exposure slightly from shot to shot.

Dragonflies can also be collected, chilled for a short period of time in a cooler or refrigerator (see "Scanning Dragonflies" below), then brought out and posed to obtain photos for use in identification. Posed shots are usually easy to recognize, and many purists frown on this type of shot *[Figure 122]*. It is, however, sometimes the only way to get composed images of some of the more uncommon or elusive species.

Camera Equipment

The 35mm single lens reflex (SLR) camera has traditionally been the favorite camera of most nature photographers. With the introduction of digital SLR cameras capable of excellent, almost grain-free photos, this is rapidly changing *[Figure 123]*. We have already converted to one of the relatively inexpensive digital SLRs, one that lets us take 6.1 megapixel images at either 72 or

A posed photo of a Dragonhunter (Hagenius brevistylus). *Photo © James L. Lasswell.*

300 dpi. The 300 dpi photos are usually of publishable quality.

The flexibility of the digital SLR cameras is fantastic. If you choose the same brand of digital camera as your old 35mm, you can use all the same lenses. You can change f-stops and shutter speeds with ease, and, in addition, you can change the ISO (the "film" speed) from shot to shot, something you simply cannot do with a 35mm SLR. These options give you a great deal of creative control over each shot you take. Memory cards (the "film") for digital SLRs are relatively expensive to buy, but they can be used over and over again, unlike 35mm film. And their large storage capacity allows the photographer to shoot a tremendous number of photos without having to worry about changing film.

Image retrieval on a digital camera is instant, and you can critique your photos and redo them immediately if they did not

{ f i g u r e 123 }

An excellent digital camera close-up of a male Blue Dasher (Pachydiplax longipennis). *Photo © John C. Seibel/John Seibel Photography.*

turn out the way you wanted. Another advantage is that the images from a digital camera can be downloaded to a computer in just a few minutes. You do not have to wait hours, or even weeks, to get your 35mm film developed. Once downloaded to the computer, the images can be manipulated, stored, and retrieved at any point in the future. With a good color printer, they can also be printed in the same format as 35mm prints without having to wait for the film to be developed while worrying about the quality of the images.

Whether your preference is the 35mm SLR camera or one of the newer digitals, it is easy to get on the Internet and look at some of the excellent pictures of dragonflies that have been taken. Many of these images have information about the cameras and lenses the photographers used to take the photos. There are also many sites that write reviews about different types of cameras and lenses. Visit these and get some feel for what you think you will need to take the kind of photos you want before visiting with a reputable camera dealer.

Digiscoping

One of the real frustrations about dragonfly photography is that you sometimes see a dragonfly you want to photograph but the closest approach you can make is well out of normal camera range. Such was the case with an encounter we had with Blue-faced Darners (*Coryphaeschna adnexa*) in south Texas *[Figure 124]*. Blue-faced Darners, which were previously reported only from Florida in the continental United States, appeared on the King Ranch in south Texas during the summer of 2002. We had the opportunity to view these beautiful creatures in August, but every one of them was flying at treetop height and when they perched it was also in the tops of the trees. They were easy

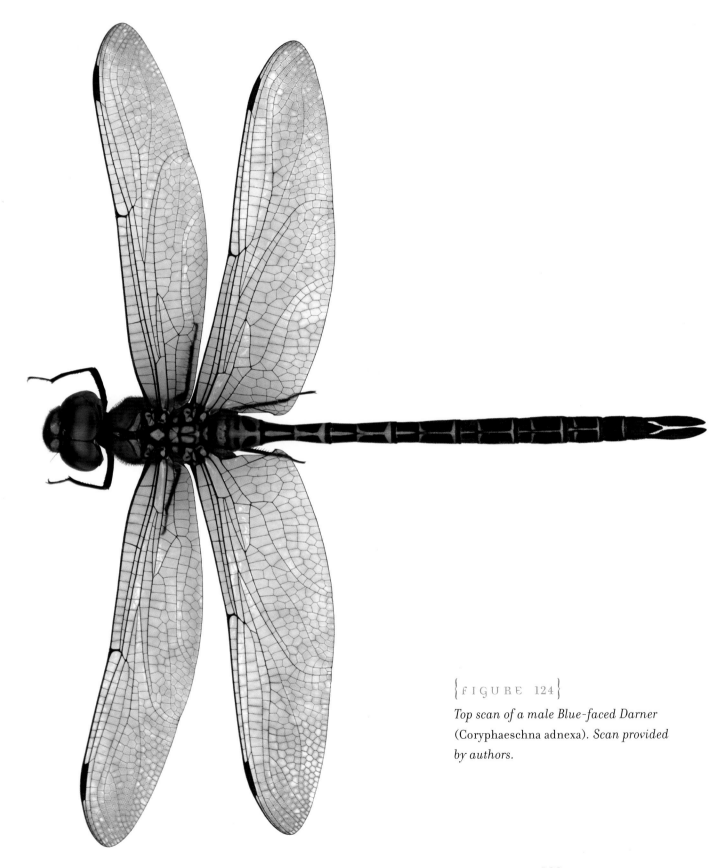

Top scan of a male Blue-faced Darner (Coryphaeschna adnexa). *Scan provided by authors.*

*A digiscope photo of a perching male Red Saddlebags (*Tramea
onusta*), a species that spends much of its time on the wing.
Photo © Bill Lindemann.*

to see through binoculars but could not be
photographed with the equipment on hand
at the time. Digiscoping would have taken
care of that problem.

Digiscoping refers to a type of photography where a digital camera connects to the
eyepiece of a field spotting scope. The spotting scope serves as a strong telephoto lens.
Adapters for attaching most fixed-lens, or
point-and-shoot, digital cameras, as well as
some makes of digital SLRs to a spotting scope
can be found on the Internet.

Digiscoping gives the photographer
the opportunity to take some excellent

photos of dragonflies without having to
worry a great deal about alarming the
intended subject—a big plus over the normal camera setup. The closest focal distance for many spotting scopes is in the
range of 15 to 20 feet. Photographing
insects this way, you do not have to worry
about scaring them away. The detail is not
as sharp as that in a photograph taken with
a close-up lens, but the results are quite
acceptable *[Figure 125]*. The only real down
side is that the equipment is very bulky and
heavy. It is not something to just pick up
and carry into the woods without a good reason (such as a Blue-faced Darner perched
in the top of a tree).

Spotting scope adapters are also available for some 35mm cameras. Again, the
spotting scope serves as a telephoto lens, but
in the case of the 35mm camera as well as
the digital SLRs, the adapters currently
require the removal of the eyepiece from
the spotting scope to attach the camera. This
results in a loss of magnification compared
with digiscoping with a point-and-shoot,
when the eyepiece is left in place. Again, a
little research into spotting scopes and how
they accommodate various cameras will
keep you up to date on the latest products.

Try It

Dragonfly photography is an extremely enjoyable and challenging hobby that affords the photographer opportunities not only to observe but also to learn about these winged creatures. As a photographer, you will discover where to find various species of dragonflies, which ones are easy to approach and which are not. You will soon know their perching habits and flight times. You will also quickly learn how to get close enough for a good photo and how to compose an artistic shot. Once you attempt dragonfly photography, you will no doubt end up taking a photo worthy of framing and hanging on the wall of your home.

The next time you go camping or walking by a lake or nearby stream, take the camera along and see if you can get a picture of a dragonfly. You will be absolutely amazed at the small yet beautiful details of nature you will notice simply by trying to find dragonflies to photograph. You will likely want to spend more and more time outdoors, enjoying not only the trees, birds, and flowers but also the less obvious creatures of nature, including (of course) the dragonflies.

Scanning Dragonflies

The falling cost of computer technology now gives dragonfly enthusiasts an alternative to photography—digital scanning of collected specimens. Flatbed scanners are capable of producing excellent, highly detailed color images, and scanning offers several possibilities. One is that a live dragonfly can be scanned and released back to the wild. Another is that a specimen collected for a museum or private collection can be scanned before it is killed. Scans provide much of the information necessary for identification, which means less handling of the specimen once it is in the collection. There is no delay in determining the quality of the scan, since it appears on the computer screen within seconds. The resulting image is in digital form and can be manipulated in several ways. It can be digitally enhanced, posted to a website, or transmitted elsewhere electronically.

There are some disadvantages, however, to the scanning technique. One problem is the large size of the files, which may be from several to many megabytes, depending on if or how the images will be printed or published. An inexpensive storage medium is the compact or video disk, especially with CD/DVD writers becoming more readily available and affordable. Another problem is that the manipulation of the live dragonfly during the scanning procedure can be very time consuming. Not all subjects are pliable, and proper positioning of the specimen is a must to obtain a good scan.

Despite these drawbacks, digital insect image collections do much of what any good collection of actual specimens does. They provide insight into the range of colors, sizes, and general anatomy of the species, and, when combined with the collection data, yield information on flight times and geographic distributions.

Materials and Methods

Computer Hardware

The biggest keys to successful scanning are a fast scanner, a fast computer, and the requisite storage capacity for the scanned images. Even though a dragonfly may be lethargic from being chilled and seemingly quiescent under a scanner cover, it will warm quickly. If it moves a wing or a leg during scanning, the movement may affect the image. Although small movements will

be practically unnoticeable, it is best to be able to scan the dragonfly as quickly as possible. Virtually all of the current computer-scanner combinations provide the speed needed to obtain quality scans.

Computer Software

Many software programs are available for image manipulation. Our suite includes Adobe Photoshop, Adobe PageMaker, and Extensis Mask Pro, but there are many others, including shareware programs, that can do this job.

Portable Scanner Hardware

During the course of each year, we spend time attending meetings or working in the field on projects not associated with dragonflies. On these trips opportunities often arise to see, photograph, and collect dragonfly species new to our collection. In the past, we collected these specimens and then just added them to the museum collection since they could not be kept alive long enough to get them back to the laboratory to scan. We solved this problem by taking a scanner and a laptop computer with us. We use 12-volt DC inverters plugged into our vehicles' cigarette lighters to operate both the scanner and computer in the field.

Miscellaneous Supplies

Although the computer equipment is the most important component of the scanning process, you will need a few other simple supplies for successful scanning. These include:

1. Collecting gear, including net and bags (see Chapter 7).

2. Can of compressed air. There are several brand names of commercially available pressurized air used to remove dust and other contaminants from hard-to-reach places on computers, printers, and other electronic equipment. Any brand may be used as long as it contains the chemical component 1,1,1,2-Tetrafluroethane. We use this to help anesthetize the dragonflies in preparation for scanning.

3. Glass cleaner and soft paper towels to keep the glass of the scanner clean. Be sure and follow the scanner manufacturer's directions in this regard.

4. A refrigerator is a must for keeping dragonflies alive. Chilling also assists in anesthetizing them prior to scanning. When in the field, take an ice chest or cooler.

5. A mouse pad with the center cut out is placed around the dragonfly on the scanner bed to prevent the scanner cover from crushing it. The confined area inside the cutaway also allows for easier orientation of the specimen, and the pad blocks stray light from the edges of the scanner. The cutaway area must be large enough to prevent the inside edges of the pad from casting shadows on the specimen. The pads we used for making the scans in this book have a cutaway area of about 115 by 140 millimeters (4.5 by 5.5 inches). It is actually best to have two separate pads, one approximately 6.5 millimeters ($\frac{1}{4}$-inch) thick and another about 9.5 millimeters ($\frac{3}{8}$-inch) thick, the latter to handle deeper bodied species such as the darners.

6. A scanning board is constructed by gluing a sheet of white felt onto a piece of stiff cardboard. It should be about the same width as the mouse pad, but a little longer.

7. A plastic ruler or similar piece of clear plastic should be at least 12 inches in length, smooth, relatively thin, and flexible.

8. Forceps help position the legs of the dragonfly prior to scanning. They should be relatively small (approximately 115 millimeters or 4.5 inches in length) and have a fine tip.

9. Like the forceps, teasing needles help position the dragonflies' legs (and wings) prior to scanning.

Scanning Procedure

Perhaps the most difficult part of the scanning procedure is the actual catching of the dragonflies. Refer to chapter seven (Collecting Dragonflies) for the collecting and post-capture handling of adult dragonflies for scanning.

Once back at the laboratory, the bags containing the specimens should be placed in the crisper portion of a household refrigerator, or in some form of rigid container on one of the shelves, where they can remain overnight. As a rule, the sooner the specimen is scanned, the better. Although short-term refrigeration has not noticeably changed the color of the dragonflies we have scanned, our current experience is limited to approximately fifty species. James Needham, Minter Westfall, and Michael May, writing in *Dragonflies of North America*, used dark cages to maintain their dragonflies without observing any changes in color, but Sidney Dunkle, in *Dragonflies of the Florida Peninsula, Bermuda, and the Bahamas*, noted the deleterious effects of freezing on specimen color and the rapid deterioration of the specimens upon thawing. Obtaining the true colors of the dragonfly works only if live specimens are scanned; freezing kills the dragonflies, and their colors change rapidly when this occurs.

Dragonflies refrigerated for thirty minutes or more are usually sedate enough to scan, but they recover very quickly. The scanning procedure must be done within a short period of time (about three minutes, depending on the species) if the dragonflies have only been under refrigeration.

Probably the best way of ensuring good scans and also ensuring the survival of the dragonflies is to scan the specimens immediately after bringing them in from the field. The key to keeping them alive for scanning and then releasing them back unharmed into the wild is to reduce the stress of handling them as much as possible.

Scanning

When getting ready to scan, select two or three of the specimens you placed into the refrigerator for safekeeping. Each of them should be in a small, clear, plastic bag. Unseal a small opening on one side of the bag. Place the plastic application tube from a canister of compressed air into the small opening, gently inflate the bag, seal it, and place it back into the refrigerator for approximately ten minutes. The combination of refrigeration and anesthesia incapacitates the dragonflies for a little longer than refrigeration alone and usually enables completion of the scanning procedure in one try.

After the selected dragonflies have been anesthetized and refrigerated for the ten-minute period, remove one of them and, with the dragonfly still in the bag, check to make sure it is not moving. Some dragonflies are more quickly anesthetized than others, so if you see any movement at all, put that one back into the refrigerator and select another. If the specimen is still, carefully remove it from the plastic bag and place it feet down on the scanning board.

We normally scan each specimen from the top and from the side *[Figures 126, 126a]*. It is best to do the top scan first because it takes much more time to position the dragonfly's legs and wings properly, and this needs to be done before it starts to wake up. After placing the dragonfly on the scanning board, use the forceps and teasing needles to gently move its legs and wings into an aesthetically pleasing, symmetrical position. Be very careful not to tear the legs or wings during this procedure.

Place the cut-out mouse pad onto the scanning board so that it surrounds but does not touch any part of the dragonfly. Next, lay the thin plastic ruler (anything thin, smooth, and somewhat flexible will work) over the dragonfly from head to tail, making sure the ruler extends past the edge of both the mouse pad and the scanning

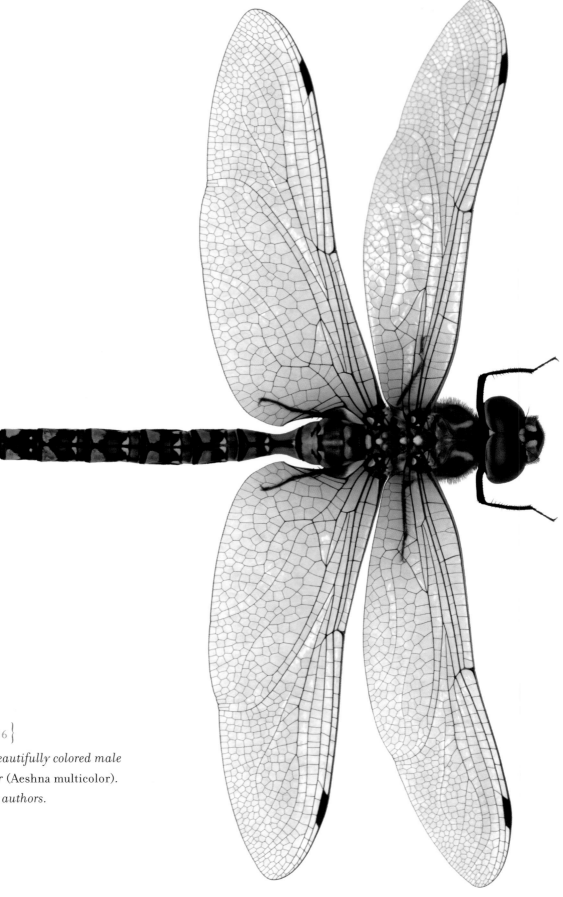

{ FIGURE 126 }

Top scan of the beautifully colored male
Blue-eyed Darner (Aeshna multicolor).
Scan provided by authors.

Side scan of the male Blue-eyed Darner
(Aeshna multicolor). Scan provided by
authors.

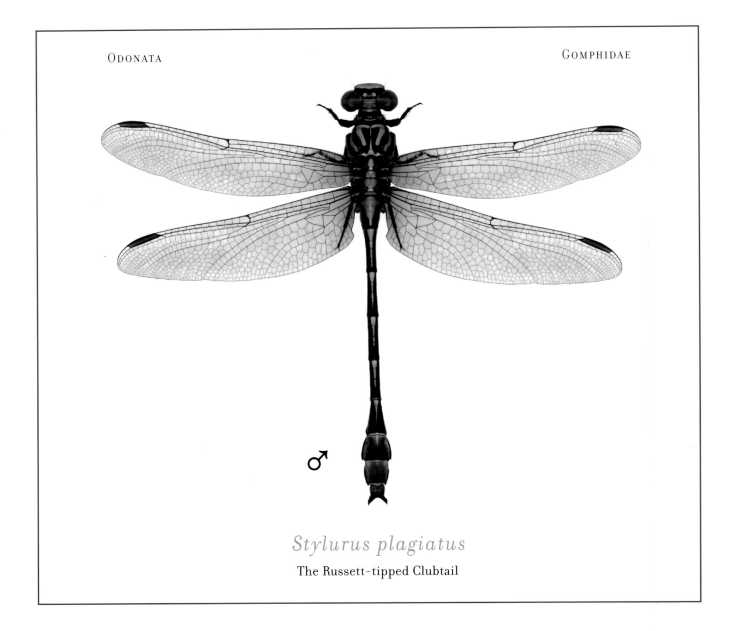

Stylurus plagiatus
The Russett-tipped Clubtail

{FIGURE 127}

*Use of a scan in a taxonomical print format
for framing and display. Although the scan
was printed much larger than life size, it lost
little resolution. Scan provided by authors.*

Pachydiplax longipennis

The Blue Dasher

{FIGURE 128}

Even a tiny Blue Dasher can be printed larger than life to bring out its beauty, including the fluorescent blue of the thorax between the wings and of the abdomen. Scan provided by authors.

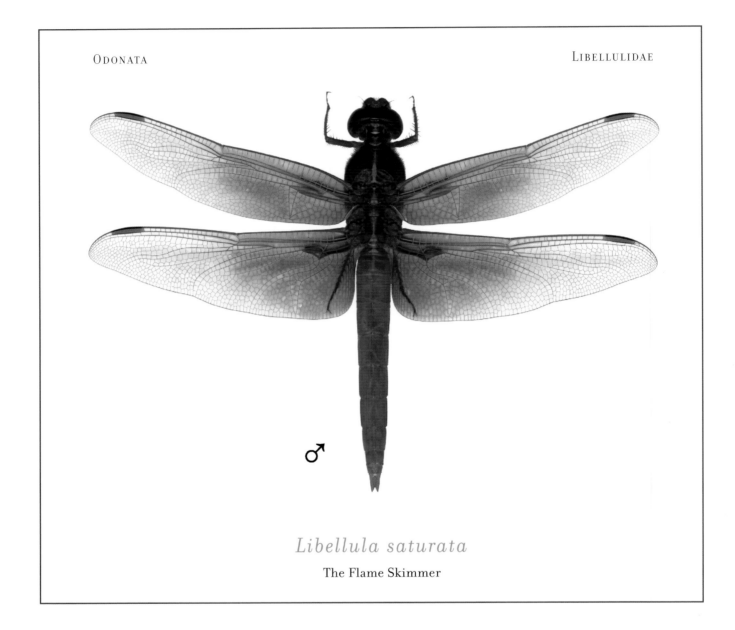

Libellula saturata

The Flame Skimmer

{FIGURE 129}

The male Flame Skimmer, a species found in the western United States, is easily recognized by the brilliant red-orange coloration of its body and the basal half of its wings. Scan provided by authors.

board. Hold the ruler in position on top of the dragonfly so that the dragonfly is wedged between the ruler and the scanning board and the mouse pad is also held in position around it. The entire apparatus can then be inverted and placed on the glass of the scanner. Do not allow the ruler, mouse pad, or scanning board to shift during this procedure lest the dragonfly's position shift also. After the apparatus is in position, release most of the pressure on the scanning board and gently remove the ruler by carefully sliding it out from between the mouse pad, dragonfly, and the glass of the scanner.

After the dragonfly is in position, scanning it at 300 dpi will normally provide a printed image that is very close to the actual size of the dragonfly. For larger, publishing quality images, scan at higher resolutions. (The larger images in this book were scanned at 1800 dpi. Higher resolutions than that picked up the movement of the dragonfly's breathing and affected the scan.) The procedure for scanning varies with the scanner make and model and with your scanning software. Check the instructions.

Once the scan is done, you might see that a leg or wing shifted during the process. With all the movement required to place the dragonfly on the scanner, it is difficult to obtain a perfectly positioned image. You can still get some very pleasing results even if a leg or wing has shifted a little. The more you practice, the faster and better at it you will become.

Compared with the dorsal, or top, scan, the side scan is easy. Simply lay the dragonfly on its side on the scanner glass and position the feet to extend below the dragonfly's thorax. The abdomen of the dragonfly should point straight back from the thorax, with the wings folded up over the dragonfly's back and the head turned for a view from the side or slightly from the top. This is all done with teasing needles, but be careful that you do not scratch the glass of the scanner or damage the dragonfly. After the dragonfly has been properly positioned, place the mouse pad around it so that it is lying flat on the glass but not touching any part of the dragonfly. Next, place the scanning board on top of the mouse pad to hold the wings in place, and then scan the dragonfly in this position.

Didymops transversa
Stream Cruiser male
length 2.24 in.
W. Feliciana Par. LA
Lake Rosemound
08 March 2003
© G.& J. Strickland 2003

To release the dragonfly after scanning, place it into a clean plastic bag and set it out at room temperature. The dragonfly will awaken from the anesthetic within five to six minutes. You can then take it to a suitable location, preferably to the site where it was collected, and let it go.

Specimens that are weakened or damaged in capture may not recover enough to fly effectively and should be placed in acetone or in a freezer and added to your collection. If you do not have or plan to keep a collection, you should make every effort to assure that the dragonflies are unharmed during both the collecting and scanning procedures and can be successfully released back to nature.

Some people have tried to scan other groups of insects with varying results. The depth of field, or focusing range, of our

{ FIGURE 130 }

A composite print assembled with image-editing software uses both scans and photographs to creatively display the Stream Cruiser (Didymops transversa). *Image © Gayle and Janell Strickland.*

scanners is about 8 millimeters (less than $\frac{1}{3}$ inch), the usual distance from the top of a pinning needle to the top of a pinned specimen. Freshly caught specimens put directly on the scanner are preferred, but some pinned specimens will work as well. The best plan is to try scanning an insect, some leaves, flowers, or whatever you want and see what happens. You will be amazed at the results.

Science and Art

If handled properly, live dragonflies can be scanned and released back to nature with no obvious damage except to their dignity. The primary purpose of scanning these insects is to create an image that matches the size and colors of each dragonfly. These images help not only to identify the dragonfly species but also to establish a number of physical characteristics common to that species. In many people's estimations, though, while the scanned images may serve worthy scientific purposes, their real value is their power to reveal the exquisite detail and astonishing beauty of dragonflies *[Figures 127-130]*.

{APPENDIX A}

DRAGONFLY WEBSITE

One of our goals for this book is to extend its usefulness through the Internet. The website Digital Dragonflies at www.dragonflies.org contains links to dragonfly scans, to the Digital Dragonfly Museum, the Damselflies of Texas, and other links of interest. These include websites, organizations, discussion lists, and publications related to dragonflies. A section devoted to the book has been added where readers may direct questions and where the answers to frequently asked questions may be found. We will place any corrections or additions to the book here along with new information of interest to readers.

{ A P P E N D I X   B }

COLLOQUIAL NAMES
OF DRAGONFLIES

Devil's horse or devil's little horse

Caballito del diablo	Spanish
Calul dracului	Romanian
Cavallo d'o demo	Portuguese
Chevau du diable	French
Devil's riding horse	English
Dickens' horse	English
Dickinson's mare	English
Dickinson's horse	English
Keval del dimoni	Spanish
Pirum hevoinen	Finnish
Pitingaul dracului	Romanian

Other references to the devil

Agent du diable	devil's agent	French
Aiguille du diable	devil's needle	French
Aspie dimonis	devil's serpent	Spanish
Bolz	devil's hammer	German
Carrozzina	devil's couch	Italian
Devil's darning needle		English
Devil's needle		English
Martai-diable	devil's hammer	French
Oni-Yamma	devil, demon dragonfly	Japanese
Pirum puka	devil's servant	Finnish
Teufelsbolz	devil's bolt, hammer	German
Teufels Grossmutter	devil's grandmother	German
Teufelsnadel	devil's needle	German
Teufelspferd	devil's bride	German

Other references to evil beings

Bruxa	witch	Spanish
Giuda	Judas	Italian
Ki-Emma	dragonfly of king of death	Japanese
Ki-Yamma	goblin dragonfly	Japanese
Magara	witch	Italian
Makre	sorcerer	French
Striga	witch	Italian
Wasserhex	water witch	German

Other references to horses

Blauspirken	little blue horse	German
Cabaleta	little horse	Portuguese
Caballito del mar	little sea horse	Spanish
Caballo del mar	sea horse	Spanish
Calul de apa	water horse	Romanian
Calul popii	priest's horse	Romanian
Calul Sf. George	St. George's horse	Romanian
Cavalo-das-bruxas	witch's horse	Portuguese
Engelspirken	angel's horse	German
Goldspierken	little golden horse	German
Gorgen Pferdlein	St. George's horse	German
Gottespferdchen	God's little horse	German
Goudpaerd	golden horse	Dutch
Hatzpferd	hunting horse	German
Himmelspferdchen	Heaven's little horse	German
Kalet de san Jaume	St. James' horse	Spanish
Kalet de sen Kames	St. James' horse	Spanish

Paerd	little horse	Dutch
Peerdeken	our dear little horse	Flemish
Pierd und Wagen	horse and wagon	German
Ritterperd	knight's horse	German
St. George's horse		English
Su yaddu e sant antoni	St. Anthony's horse	Italian
Vrouwpeerd	Madonna's horse	Flemish

References to sharp instruments (needles, pins, swords, knives, arrows, etc.)

Aiguillette	needle or pin	French
Ching-t'ing	greenish pointed thing	Chinese
Ciseau	knife-like	French
Cisette	knife-like	French
Gluftenschisser	needle	German
Guge	needle	Italian
Guzela	little needle	Italian
Jungfruslanda	fairy spinning needle	Swedish
Matassaire	needle	Italian
Mattassaro	needle	Italian
Pina'o	pin fly	Hawaiian
Saiton	arrow	Italian
Scharenschliffer	knife-like	German
Schillenbold	shooting needle, arrow	German
Schurnadel	shearing needle	German
Siton	arrow	Italian
Spendel	shooting needle	German
Spillebold	shooting needle, arrow	German
Spilleschisser	shooting needle	German
Spullet	little pin, needle	Italian
Trollslanda	fairy spinning needle	Swedish
Ziton	arrow	Italian

References to harm to humans

Augenstecher	eye sticker	German
Cavo-ue	eye sticker	French
Ciapacavei	to mess up hair	Italian
Creve-oeil	eye sticker	French
Kehlstecher	eye sticker	German
Lleva-dits	finger cutter	Spanish

Ogensteker	eye sticker	German
Ogenstuater	eye sticker	German
Orestikker	ear shooter, sticker	Norwegian
Ore-snelde	ear shooter, sticker	Norwegian
Ore-sting	ear shooter, sticker	Norwegian
Pakh-araille	ear piercer	French
Pisse-en-z'yeux	shoot poison into the eye	French
Rodadits	finger gnawer	Spanish
Taglia faccia	to cut the face	Italian
Taglia-naso	to cut the nose	Italian
Tajafacc	to cut the face	Italian
Talla-campanas	to cut the face	Italian
Tallanassos	nostril cutter	Spanish
Tira-olhos	eye sticker	Portuguese
Tire-z-yeux	shoot poison into the eye	French

References to damage to animals

Amattsasomare	ass killer	Italian
Ammazza-cavalli	horse killer, sticker	Italian
Bullenbiter	bull biter, stinger	German
Bullstang	bull stinger	English
Horse-long-cripple	cripples horse	English
Hoss-stinger	horse stinger	English
Matacaballos	horse killer	Spanish
Matsakavats	horse killer	Italian
Pferdstecher	horse sticker	German

References to snakes

Adder bolt	snake spear	English
Adderfly	snake fly	English
Ather-cap	snake with a head	English
Cap-de-sur	serpent's head	French
Damhan nathac	bull snake	Scottish
Fisso-serp	serpent's head	French
Fleeing snake		English
Flying adder		English
Nattarhalter	snake attacker	German
Penny adder	small snake	English
Pfaffen kochin	priest's serpent, servant	German
Pfaffen wip	priest's serpent, servant	German

Pico-serp	serpent's head	French
Snake doctor		English
Snake feeder		English
Snake-stang	snake bolt, spear	English
Serpens	serpent, snake	Spanish
Tarbh-nathrac	bull snake	Scottish

Descriptive names of people

Capelan	chaplain	French
Ciavatin	shoemaker	Italian
Couturiere	dressmaker (needle)	French
Dame de Paris	well-dressed lady	French
Donzella	little gentleman	Portuguese
Ferero	blacksmith, ironworker	Spanish
Mariee	young married woman	French
Moine	monk	French
Moungeto	little nun	French
Pretre	priest	French
Reine	the queen	French
Sinoriko	young man, gentleman	Spanish
Snidr	tailor (needle)	German

References to water nymphs, guardians, etc.

Cura-pess	keeper of the fish	Italian
Froschenhueter	guardian of the water	German
Gardo d'aigo	guardian of the water	French
Guarda-cibbia	guard of the tubs	Italian
Guarda-pescher	fisher guard	Italian
Guardian del pozzo	guardian of the moat	Italian
Marca-agua	observer of the water	Italian
Nymphe	water spirit	French
Passalakwa	water passer	Italian
Re d'acqua	king of the water	Italian
Scalus de apa	water cricket	Romanian
Schleiferglasser	water glider	German
Vattenjungfer	water nymph	Swedish
Wasserbumme	water hummer	German
Wasserjungfer	water nymph	German
Wasserjungfern	water nymph	German
Wassermann	spirit of the water	German

Wasserpfrau	water peacock	German
Water butterfly		English
Waterjuffer	water nymph, naiad	Dutch
Waterjuffertje	water nymph, naiad	Dutch

References to animals

Cura-pess	keeper of the fish	Italian
Grilli	cricket	Italian
Himmelsziege	sky goat	German
Holtpirken	woodpecker	German
Ka-Tombo	mosquito dragonfly	Japanese
Kingfisher	name of a bird	English
Mosca	fly	Spanish
Mosquito hawk		English
Mouron	salamander	French
Parot	butterfly	Spanish
Peacock		English
Pfaufliege	peacock fly	German
Poule d'eau	water wagtail (a bird)	French
Ridda	black cricket	Italian
Rillu	black cricket	Italian
Rilo	black cricket	Italian
Scalus de apa	water cricket	Romanian
Wasserpfrau	water peacock	German

Others

Aka-Tombo	red dragonfly	Japanese
Akitsu	dragonfly, ancient name	Japanese
Akitsu-mushi	autumn insect	Japanese
Beni-Tombo	pink dragonfly	Japanese
Ching-t'ing	green streak	Chinese
Cousin	refers to large species	French
Doublet	refers to four wings	French
Dragonfly		English
Glaser	wings easily destroyed	German
Glasermaker	wings easily destroyed	German
Impistun	pounder, pestle	Italian
Kino-Tombo	yellow dragonfly	Japanese
Ko-Yamma-Tombo	little mountain dragonfly	Japanese
Kuro-Yamma-Tombo	black mountain dragonfly	Japanese

*Libelinha	book-like or balance scale?	Portuguese		Pistun del awa	pounder of the water	Italian
*Libellen	book-like or balance scale?	German		Plattbauch	flat belly (genus *Anax*)	German
*Libelle	book-like or balance scale?	German		Rota-cribbie	fly around the tubs	Italian
*Libellule	book-like or balance scale?	French		Roumpo-veire	glass breaker	French
*Libel	book-like	Dutch		Shiokara-Tombo	salt-fish dragonfly	Japanese
*Libellula	level or balance scale	Italian		Shorai-Tombo	dragonfly of the dead	Japanese
*Libelula	level or balance scale	Spanish		Shoryo-Tombo	dragonfly of ancestors	Japanese
Ma-lang	dragonfly	Chinese		Silverpin	refers to metallic beauty	English
Mugiwara-Tombo	wheat-straw dragonfly	Japanese		T'ong-me	dragonfly	Chinese
Pastapistun	pounder, pestle	Italian		Tanilai'	dragonfly	Navajo
Perle	pearl	German		Tombo	non-aeshnids	Japanese
Pisimfontana	urinates in the fountain	Italian		Yamma	aeshnids	Japanese
Pistapistun	pounder, pestle	Italian		Yamma-Tombo	mountain dragonfly	Japanese

Footnote (*see page 27*):

*Libel is from the Latin libellus meaning little book or pamphlet.

*Libella is from the Latin libra, meaning balance. It refers to a small balance or leveling tool.

THE DRAGONFLY SOCIETY OF THE AMERICAS COLLECTING STATEMENT

Statement of Committee on Collecting Policy

A final draft of the DSA Collecting Guidelines has been completed through the diligent work of the Committee set up by George Harp, chaired by Richard Orr, and with the valuable comments of many of our members. This draft is basically the draft published in ARGIA (1994, vol. 6, no. 3, pp. 6-8), but with a few significant changes.

Preamble

Our ethical responsibility to assess and preserve natural resources, for the maintenance of biological diversity in perpetuity, and for the increase of knowledge requires that Odonatologists examine the rationale and practices of collecting Odonata, for the purpose of governing their own activities. While we recognize that historically most threats to preservation of odonate species have been a consequence of habitat destruction, we believe that there is a need for responsible collecting practices. To this end, the following guidelines are outlined, based on these premises:

0.1 Odonata are a natural resource.

0.2 Any human interaction with a natural resource (e.g. Odonata and their environment) should be in a manner not harmful to the perpetuation of that resource.

0.3 The collection of Odonata:

- 0.31 is a means of introducing children and adults to awareness and study of their natural environment;

- 0.32 has an essential role in gathering of scientific information including the advancement of taxonomic knowledge, both for its own sake and as a basis from which to develop rational means for protecting the environment, and maintaining the health of the biosphere;

- 0.33 is an enjoyable educational or scientific activity which can generally be pursued in a manner not detrimental to the resource (e.g. Odonata and their environment) involved.

Guidelines

Purposes of Collecting (consistent with the above):

1.1 To create a reference collection for study and appreciation.

1.2 To document regional diversity, frequency and variability of species, and as voucher material for published records.

1.3 To document faunal representation in environments undergoing or threatened with alteration by human or natural forces.

1.4 To participate in development of regional checklists and institutional reference collections.

1.5 To complement a planned research endeavor.

1.6 To aid in dissemination of educational information.

1.7 To provide material for taxonomic studies.

1.8 To provide information for ecological studies.

Restraints As To Numbers:

2.1 Collection (of adults or of immature stages) should be limited to sampling, not depleting, the population concerned; numbers collected should be consistent with, and not excessive for, the purpose of the collecting.

2.2 When collecting where the extent and/or fragility of the population is unknown, caution and restraint should be exercised.

Collecting Methods:

3.1 Field collecting should be selective and should minimize harm to non-target organisms.

Live Material:

4.1 Rearing to elucidate life histories and to obtain series of immature stages and adults is encouraged, provided that collection of the rearing stock is in keeping with the guidelines.

4.2 Reared material in excess of need should be released, but only in the region where it originated, and in suitable habitat.

4.3 Because of such concerns as introduction of disease and adverse redistribution of genetic resources, release of excess reared material is not encouraged unless it is done in conjunction with a planned restoration program, and under supervision of knowledgeable biologists.

Environmental and Legal Considerations:

5.1 Protecting the supporting habitat must be recognized as essential to the protection of a species.

5.2 Collecting should be performed in a manner such as to minimize trampling or other damage to the habitat.

5.3 Property rights and sensibilities of others must be respected (including those of nature photographers and observers).

5.4 All collecting must be in compliance with regulations relating to public lands (such as state and national parks, monuments, recreational areas, etc.) and to individual species and habitats.

5.5 Importation and movement of exotic species must be in compliance with international, national, or regional laws prior to importing live or dead material.

Responsibility For Collected Material:

6.1 All material should be preserved with full data attached, including parentage of immatures when known.

6.2 All material should be protected from physical damage and deterioration, as by light, molds, and museum pests.

6.3 Collections should be made available for examination by qualified researchers.

6.4 Collections or specimens, and their associated written, electronic, photographic and other records, should be willed or offered to the care of an appropriate scientific institution, if the collector lacks space or loses interest, or anticipates death.

6.5 Type specimens, especially holotypes or allotypes, should be deposited in appropriate institutions.

Related Activities Of Collectors:

7.1 Collecting should include permanently recorded field notes regarding habitat, conditions, and other pertinent information.

7.2 Recording of observations of behavior and of biological interactions should be encouraged and receive as high a priority as collecting.

7.3 Photographic records, with full data, are also encouraged.

7.4 Education of the public about collecting and conservation, as reciprocally beneficial activities, should be undertaken whenever possible.

Traffic In Odonata Specimens:

8.1 Collections of specimens for exchange should be performed in accordance with these guidelines.

8.2 Rearing of specimens for exchange should be from stock obtained in a manner consistent with these guidelines, and so documented.

8.3 The sale of individual specimens or the mass collection of Odonata for commercial purposes (e.g. fish bait), and collection or use of specimens for creation of salable artifacts, are not included among the purposes of the Dragonfly Society of the Americas.

(From http://www.afn.org/~iori/oincolgl.html)

{APPENDIX D}

MONITORING DRAGONFLY MIGRATION

(Based on the Pacific Northwest Dragonfly Migration Project flight data form)

Today's date

Date of flight (if not today)

Location of flight (please be specific)

Latitude

Longitude (if known)

Time of migration

From   To

Was the migration still in progress when you stopped observing?

Yes   No

Height of flight

Max   Min

Weather

Cloud cover (estimate percent cover)

Wind direction

Wind from the

Measured

Estimated

Wind speed (mph)

Measured

Estimated

Temperature

Measured

Estimated

Personal information

Your name

Street address

City

State

Zip code

Phone number

E-mail address

Flight information

Flight direction (vanishing point bearing)

Measured with compass?

Otherwise estimated (specify)

Magnetic North?   True North?

Description of dragonflies

Describe your observations in as much detail as you want (use back of form if necessary) to help us identify the species.

Species of dragonflies suspected by Russell et al. 1998 to be migratory include:

Family Aeshnidae

Lance-tipped Darner (*Aeshna constricta*)

Lake Darner (*Aeshna eremita*)

Shadow Darner (*Aeshna umbrosa*)

Common Green Darner (*Anax junius*)

Swamp Darner (*Epiaeschna heros*)

Family Libellulidae

Calico Pennant (*Celithemis elisa*)

Seaside Dragonlet (*Erythrodiplax berenice*)

Eastern Pondhawk (*Erythemis simplicicollis*)

Bar-winged Skimmer (*Libellula axilena*)

Twelve-spotted Skimmer (*Libellula pulchella*)

Four-spotted Skimmer (*Libellula quadrimaculata*)

Painted Skimmer (*Libellula semifasciata*)

Great Blue Skimmer (*Libellula vibrans*)

Hyacinth Glider (*Miathyria marcella*)

Blue Dasher (*Pachydiplax longipennis*)—possibly a regular migrant in small numbers

Wandering Glider (*Pantala flavescens*)

Spot-winged Glider (*Pantala hymenaea*)

Ruby Meadowhawk (*Sympetrum rubicundulum*)

White-faced Meadowhawk (*Sympetrum obtrusum*)

Yellow-legged Meadowhawk (*Sympetrum vicinum*)

Variegated Meadowhawk (*Sympetrum corruptum*)

Black Saddlebags (*Tramea lacerata*)

Carolina Saddlebags (*Tramea carolina*)

Vermilion Saddlebags (*Tramea abdominalis*)

Striped Saddlebags (*Tramea calverti*)

Red Saddlebags (*Tramea onusta*)

{BOOKSHELF}

Regional Field Guides and Checklists

Start here if one of these guides covers your area.

Beckmeyer, Roy J., and Donald G. Huggins. 1998. *Checklist of Kansas Dragonflies.* Emporia State University.

Biggs, Kathy. 2000. *Common Dragonflies of California: A Beginner's Pocket Guide.* Sebastopol, Calif.: Azalea Creek Publishing.

Bocanegra, Omar R. 2002. *A Field Guide to the Dragonflies of the Fort Worth Nature Center and Refuge.* Published by Omar R. Bocanegra.

Cannings, Rob A., and Kathleen M. Stuart. 1977. *The Dragonflies of British Columbia.* B. C. Prov. Museum Handbook 35.

Carpenter, Virginia. 1991. *Dragonflies and Damselflies of Cape Cod.* Brewster: Cape Cod Museum of Natural History.

Curry, James R. 2001. *Dragonflies of Indiana.* Indiana Academy of Science.

Dunkle, Sidney W. 1989. *Dragonflies of the Florida Peninsula, Bermuda, and the Bahamas.* Gainesville: Scientific Publishers.

Garman, Philip. 1927. The Odonata or Dragonflies of Connecticut. Part V. *Guide to the Insects of Connecticut.* Connecticut Geological and Natural History Survey Bulletin 39. (This book is occasionally sold on eBay and should be used along with a modern reference.)

Legler, Karl, Dorothy Legler, and Dave Westover. 1998. *Color Guide to Common Dragonflies of Wisconsin.* Sauk City, Wis. (Dave Westover is a contributor to this volume and many of his photos may be found here.)

Manolis, Tim. 2003. *Dragonflies and Damselflies of California.* Berkeley: University of California Press.

Paulson, Dennis R. 1999. *Dragonflies of Washington.* Seattle Audubon Society.

Rosche, Larry. 2002. *Dragonflies and Damselflies of Northeast Ohio.* Cleveland: Cleveland Museum of Natural History.

Recommended General Reference Works

Corbet, Philip S. 1999. *Dragonflies: Behavior and Ecology of Odonata.* Ithaca: Cornell University Press. (This is the most complete reference on the topic. Any serious student of dragonflies and damselflies should own a copy.)

Corbet, Philip S., Cynthia Longfield, and Norman W. Moore. 1960. *Dragonflies.* London: Collins. (An older work, it still contains relevant information.)

Dunkle, Sidney W. 2000. *Dragonflies through Binoculars: A Field Guide to Dragonflies of North America.* New York: Oxford University Press. (The first illustrated field guide to all the U. S. dragonflies includes color photos and distribution maps for each species.)

Inoue, Kiyoshi, and Kôzô Tani. 1999. *All about Dragonflies.* Osaka, Japan: Tombow Publishing Co. (Written in Japanese with some English annotations, this book covers all the dragonflies and damselflies in Japan. It is illustrated with beautiful color photos taken by the authors.)

Needham, James G., Minter J. Westfall, Jr., and Michael L. May. 2000. *Dragonflies of North America.* Gainesville: Scientific Publishers. (This book is a revision of the original 1955 edition, *A Manual of the Dragonflies of North America (Anisoptera)* [University of California Press] by the first two authors, and includes some color plates. A technical treatise, it is the most detailed work on the taxonomy of North American dragonflies.)

Nikula, Blair, Donald Stokes, Jackie Sones, and Lillian W. Stokes. 2002. *Stokes Beginner's Guide to Dragonflies.* New York: Little, Brown. (A good introductory book for learning about dragonflies.)

Silsby, Jill. 2001. *Dragonflies of the World.* Washington, D. C.: Smithsonian Institution Press. (The first work to illustrate both dragonflies and damselflies from around the world, this book has excellent photos, descriptions, and general information.)

Walker, Edmund M. 1953, 1958. *The Odonata of Canada and Alaska.* 2 Vols. Toronto: University Toronto Press.

Walker, Edmund M., and Philip S. Corbet. 1975. *The Odonata of Canada and Alaska.* Vol. 3. Toronto: University of Toronto Press. (This classic three-volume set was recently reprinted. The books are very detailed and technical, and not meant for the casual reader.)

References

CHAPTER 1 *The World of Dragonflies*

Dunkle, Sidney W. 1989. *Dragonflies of the Florida Peninsula, Bermuda, and the Bahamas*. Gainesville: Scientific Publishers.

The Tree of Life Web Project. A collaborative Internet project containing information about phylogeny and biodiversity. http://tolweb.org/tree/phylogeny.html

CHAPTER 2 *Dragonfly Tales*

Bergen, Fanny D. 1969. *Animal and Plant Lore: Collected from the Oral Tradition of English Speaking People*. New York: Kraus Reprint.

Bird, Allison. 1992. *Heart of the Dragonfly: Historical Development of the Cross Necklaces of the Pueblo and Navajo Peoples*. Albuquerque: University of New Mexico Press.

Campbell, Charles A. R. 1925. *Bats, Mosquitoes, and Dollars*. Boston: Stratford.

Cushing, Frank Hamilton. 1975. *Zuni Breadstuff*. New York: AMS Press.

D'Aguilar, Jacques, Jean-Louis Dommanget, and Rene Prechac. *A Field Guide to the Dragonflies of Britain, Europe and North Africa*. London: Collins.

Davis, F. Hadland. Reprint edition, 1992. *Myths and Legends of Japan*. New York: Dover Publications.

Fansler, Dean S. 1965. *Filipino Popular Tales*. Hattsboro: Folklore Associates.

Farmer, John Stephen. 1971. *Americanisms—Old and New*. Ann Arbor: Gryphon Books.

Grimm, J. 1961. *Folk-lore and Fable: Aesop, Grimm, Andersen*. New York: Collier.

Halliwell-Phillipps, James O. 1889. *A Dictionary of Archaic and Provincial Words, Obsolete Phrases, Proverbs, and Ancient Customs, from the Fourteenth Century*. London: Reeves and Turner, pp. 164–797.

Hearn, Lafcadio. 1901. *A Japanese Miscellany*. Boston: Little, Brown, pp. 81–121.

Henry, Teuira. 1971. *Ancient Tahiti*. New York: Kraus Reprint.

Hillerman, Tony. 1986. *The Boy Who Made Dragonfly: A Zuni Myth*. Albuquerque: University of New Mexico Press.

Liu, Wu-Chi, and Irving Yucheng Lo. 1975. *Sunflower Splendor: Three Thousand Years of Chinese Poetry*. Bloomington and London: Indiana University Press.

MacCulloch, J. A. 1964. *Eddic (mythology)*. New York: Cooper Square.

Matthews, Washington. 1994. *Navajo Legends*. Salt Lake City: University of Utah Press.

Mayer, Fanny Hagin. 1985. *Ancient Tales in Modern Japan: An Anthology of Japanese Folk Tales*. Bloomington: Indiana University Press.

Rodanas, Kristina. 1991. *Dragonfly's Tale*. New York: Clarion Books.

Sarot, Eden Emanuel. 1958. *Folklore of the Dragonfly: A Linguistic Approach*. Roma: Edizioni Di Storia E Letteratura.

Sato, Hiroaki, and Burton Watson. 1981. *From the Country of Eight Islands*. Garden City, N. Y.: Anchor/Doubleday.

Williams, Charles A. S. 1974. *Outlines of Chinese Symbolism and Art Motives: An Alphabetical Compendium of Antique Legends and Beliefs, as Reflected in the Manners and Customs of the Chinese*. New York: Dover Publications.

CHAPTER 3 *The Prehistory of Dragonflies*

Barthel, K. Werner. 1990. *Solnhofen, a study in Mesozoic paleontology*. Translated and revised by N. H. M. Swinburne. Edited by S. C. Morris. New York: Cambridge University Press.

Carpenter, Frank M. 1992. Arthropoda 4. Part R, Vol. 3: Superclass Hexapoda. In *Treatise on Invertebrate Paleontology*. R. C. Moore, ed. New York: Geological Society of America.

Grimaldi, David. 2001. Insect evolutionary history from Handlirsch to Hennig and beyond. *Journal of Paleontology* 75(6):1152–1160.

Maisey, John G., ed. 1991. *Santana Fossils: An Illustrated Atlas*. Neptune City, N. J.: T. F. H. Publications.

National Center for Biotechnology Information. GenBank. http://www.ncbi.nlm.nih.gov

Wang, J. 1998. Scientists flock to explore China's "site of the century." *Science* 279:1626–1627.

Wootten, R. J., J. Kukalova-Peck, D. J. S. Newman, and J. Muzon. 1998. Smart engineering in the mid-Carboniferous: How well could Paleozoic dragonflies fly? *Science* 282:749–751.

Zhang, Junfeng. 1999. Aeschnidiid nymphs from the Jehol biota (latest Jurassic-early Cretaceous), China, with a discussion of the family Aeschnidiidae (Insecta, Odonata). *Cretaceous Research* 20:813–827.

CHAPTER 4 *Dragonfly Lives*

Corbet, Philip S. 1999. *Dragonflies: Behavior and Ecology of Odonata*. Ithaca, New York: Cornell University Press.

Dunkle, S. W. 1984. Head damage due to mating in *Ophiogomphus* dragonflies (Anisoptera: Gomphidae). *Notulae Odonatologicae* 2:63–64.

Hofslund, P. B. 1977. Dragonfly attacks and kills a Ruby-throated Hummingbird. *Loon* 49:238.

Merritt, Richard W., and Kenneth W. Cummins, eds. 1984. *An Introduction to the Aquatic Insects of North America*. 2d ed. DuBuque, Ia.: Kendall/Hunt Publishing Co.

Needham, James G., and Minter J. Westfall, Jr. 1955. *A Manual of the Dragonflies of North America (Anisoptera)*. Berkeley: University of California Press.

Pritchard, G. 1986. The operation of the labium in larval drag-
    onflies. *Odonatologica* 15(4):451.

Sherk, T. E. 1977. Development of the compound eye of drag-
    onflies (Odonata). I. Larval compound eyes. *Journal of
    Experimental Zoology* 201:391–416.

Sherk, T. E. 1978a. Development of the compound eye of drag-
    onflies (Odonata). II. Development of the larval compound
    eyes. *Journal of Experimental Zoology* 203:47–60.

Sherk, T. E. 1978b. Development of the compound eye of drag-
    onflies (Odonata). III. Adult compound eyes. *Journal of
    Experimental Zoology* 203:61–80.

Sherk, T. E. 1978c. Development of the compound eye of drag-
    onflies (Odonata). IV. Development of the adult com-
    pound eyes. *Journal of Experimental Zoology* 203:183–200.

Westneat, M. W., O. Betz, R. W. Blob, K. Fezzaa, W. J.
    Cooper, and W-k. Lee. 2003. Tracheal respiration in
    insects visualized with synchrotron X-ray imaging. *Science*
    299:558–560.

CHAPTER 5 *The Natural History of Dragonflies*

Calvert, P. 1947. How many mosquito larvae and pupae are
    required to make one dragonfly? *Proceedings of the Entomological
    Society of Washington* 49(6):171–172.

Corbet, Philip. S. 1999. *Dragonflies: Behavior and Ecology of Odonata.*
    Ithaca: Cornell University Press.

Lincoln, E. 1940. Growth in *Aeshna tuberculifera* (Odonata).
    Proceedings of the American Philosophical Society 83(5):589–605.

Monarch Watch. The University of Kansas Entomology
    Program. www.monarchwatch.org

Russell, R. W., M. L. May, K. L. Soltesz, and J. W. Fitzpatrick.
    1998. Massive swarm migrations of dragonflies (Odonata)
    in eastern North America. *American Midland Naturalist*
    140(2):325–342.

Sarot, Eden Emanuel. 1958. *Folklore of the Dragonfly: A Linguistic
    Approach.* Roma: Edizioni Di Storia E Letteratura.

Trottier, R. 1971. Effect of temperature on the life cycle of
    Anax junius (Odonata: Aeshnidae) in Canada. *Canadian
    Entomologist* 103:1671–1683.

CHAPTER 6 *Watching Dragonflies*

Dunkle, Sidney W. 1989. *Dragonflies of the Florida Peninsula, Bermuda,
    and the Bahamas.* Gainesville: Scientific Publishers.

Dunkle, Sidney W. 2000. *Dragonflies through Binoculars: A Field Guide
    to Dragonflies of North America.* New York: Oxford University Press.

Needham, James G., Minter J. Westfall, Jr., and Michael L. May. 2000.
    Dragonflies of North America. Gainesville: Scientific Publishers.

Silsby, Jill. 2001. *Dragonflies of the World.* Washington, D.C.:
    Smithsonian Institution Press.

University of Puget Sound James R. Slater Museum of
    Natural History. Odonata: Dragonfly Biodiversity.
    http://www.ups.edu/biology/museum/UPSdragonflies.html

CHAPTER 7 *Collecting Dragonflies*

Dunkle, Sidney W. 1989. *Dragonflies of the Florida Peninsula, Bermuda,
    and the Bahamas.* Gainesville: Scientific Publishers.

Merritt, Richard W., and Kenneth W. Cummins, eds. 1997.
    An Introduction to the Aquatic Insects of North America. Dubuque, Ia.:
    Kendall/Hunt Publishing Company.

Mitchell, F. L., and J. L. Lasswell. 2000. Digital dragonflies.
    American Entomologist 46(2):110–115.

CHAPTER 8 *Water Gardening for Dragonflies*

Mitchell, Forrest L. 1998. Flying Dragons in the Backyard. *Helen
    Nash's Pond & Garden* 1(1):30–35.

Mitchell, F. L., and J. L. Lasswell. Forthcoming. Population char-
    acteristics of the dragonfly *Pantala flavescens* colonizing small ponds
    constructed for water quality research. *Southwestern Entomologist.*

CHAPTER 9 *Picturing Dragonflies*

Digital Dragonflies. http://www.dragonflies.org

Dunkle, Sidney W. 1989. *Dragonflies of the Florida Peninsula, Bermuda,
    and the Bahamas.* Gainesville: Scientific Publishers.

Mitchell, F. L., and J. L. Lasswell. 2000. Digital dragonflies.
    American Entomologist 46(2):110–115.

Needham, James G., Minter J. Westfall, Jr., and Michael L.
    May. 2000. *Dragonflies of North America.* Gainesville: Scientific
    Publishers.

{ACKNOWLEDGMENTS}

The authors thank the many friends and colleagues who have helped with various aspects of the book over the years that it has taken to assemble. One of the most satisfying parts of working with dragonflies is meeting all the enthusiastic people who share our delight and interest in these remarkable insects. We have had a lot of help and support from a lot of people and there is a definite risk of leaving someone out that should be included, we apologize if we have. It is also not an attempt to spread the blame for any errors of fact or omission, which are hopefully few in number. Those belong solely to us.

Photographers Robert Behrstock, Greg Lasley, Bill Lindemann, Jack Brady, John Seibel, Mitsutoshi Sugimura, Dave Westover, Curtis Williams, Lee Hovey King, Larissa Heimer, and Anne Goldstein were kind enough to grant us use of their work. The assistance of colleagues John Abbott, Takashi Aoki, Chris Durden, Sidney Dunkle, Gordon Hutchings, Kiyoshi Inoue, Jarmila Kukalova-Peck, Tom Langschied, John Oswald, and Dennis Paulson has been invaluable. Special thanks go to Clay Helms and the staff of Our-Town Internet Service who have supported the Digital Dragonflies Project from the very first day in July 1996.

We are especially grateful to all the many staff members and students who have worked on the project over the years. Numerous students have been taught web design and Internet protocols using the dragonfly websites as teaching tools and all of them have helped us improve our work.

We thank our editor, Shannon Davies, for helping turn our writing into something readable and Cathleen Elliott for the beautiful jacket and book design. Thanks also to Peter N. Névraumont for never despairing of us, and to the Texas A&M University Press for the warm welcome we received.

Finally, we thank our families for putting up with us during the various trips and trials we have gone through during our journey and hope that our children, Laurie Rodriguez, Jamie Lasswell, Robert Mitchell and Evelyn Mitchell are proud of the result.

{INDEX}

Glenelg Country School
12793 Folly Quarter Road
Glenelg, Maryland 21737